GARLIC CLOVES

& Red Underwear

GARLIC CLOVES
& Red
Underwear

Story Copyright © 2022 by: Joseph L. Cacibauda
Copy Editor: Tiziano T. Dossena
Cover Design and Interior Layout: Dominic A. Campanile

Copyright © 2022 Idea Graphics, LLC • Port St. Lucie, FL
All rights reserved.

ISBN: 978-1-948651-36-3
Library of Congress Control Number: 2022907117
Published by: Idea Press (*an imprint of Idea Graphics, LLC*) — Florida, USA
www.ideapress-usa.com
Administrative Office, Florida, USA • email: ideapress33@gmail.com
Editorial Office, New York, USA • editoreusa@gmail.com

Printed in the USA - 1st Edition, May 2022

JOSEPH L. CACIBAUDA

GARLIC CLOVES & Red Underwear

ORIGINS OF FAMILIAR
ITALIAN CUSTOMS AND ADMONITIONS

I dedicate this writing to all of those
Facebook Sicilian and Italian group members
and emailed colleagues who responded to my call
for familiar sayings and beliefs that they
remembered hearing growing up.

It is also dedicated to readers who might pick up this book
because they are curious to learn more about these great cultures.

GARLIC CLOVES
& RED UNDERWEAR

• •

Garlic for Italians is the chicken soup for the Jewish. Both are catch-all remedies for what ails you. The reader won't find chicken soup mentioned here, but will see garlic referenced for a host of cures and protections. Another familiar protection is the color red. In the Indian Vedanta culture, red is associated with the first energy center of the body (chakra). There are seven chakras that furnish energy to the body and this red colored chakra is centered at the base of the spine. The base of the spine is the foundation of the system, thus a grounding energy that when activated fortifies the nervous system to naturally allow organs and glands to send out appropriate elements to protect and heal the body. Whether one is familiar with this concept, or believes in such an idea, the use of red to ward off bad spirits (energies i.e., the evil eye) probably migrated from India to the west. The red underwear in the title refers to the old custom of wearing red underwear over-night from New Year's Eve to New Year's Day.

INTRODUCTION

● ●

ORIGINS of FAMILIAR ITALIAN
CUSTOMS AND ADMONITIONS

This is the work of over 300 hundred authors. In fact, their contributions are based on the knowledge and beliefs from their parents, grandparents, uncles, and aunts, which exponentially increases the number of writers that must be credited here. Following my call-out to Facebook Italian and Sicilian group members for "old Italian superstitions and cures" they heard growing up, I received a number of rich and interesting replies. We are apt to call their contributions "superstitious" because these prescriptions and proscriptions to our modern, shall I say sophisticated and educated senses seem to be the stuff of woo woo twilight zone realms. But, in fairness to our ancestors, those that believed and applied these sayings, we have few rights to look at these ideas with disdain, with the arrogance of wiser minds, and self-sure these practices are all "superstitions."

These sayings and beliefs have ancient roots passed along through many regions for thousands of years and generations. They have surely worked at some level or some degree to have undergone these migrations and survive their extinctions. Could it be with all of our learning and luxuries that we have missed the nature of truths behind these axioms and practices?

Perhaps the following writer's sentiment is more accurate than we care to admit: "...I think in some ways the primitive peoples, with their swift subconscious intuition and their minds unclouded by mere book knowledge, perceived truths to which we moderns are blind" (Carpenter).

Along the years, science has produced results that often lend credence to many things old-country folks have known all along. Modern societies consider folk remedies to be superstitions until science validates their efficacies through experiments. For example, scientific studies of the brain show that its left side controls the body's right side, and the brain's right side controls the body's left side. In most old-time maxims, the right side is presumed to be the favored side, producing positive results. The left side is said to produce the opposite results. In the adages, "If your right ear itches, someone is saying something nice about you. If your right eye itches, a pleasant surprise awaits you. If your right palm itches, money will soon come to you." Brain studies conclude that the left brain/right side is used for speech and logical tasks including calculating and performing math. A right-hand itch could unknowingly stimulate the calculating/logical left brain to intuitively make decisions that could increase one's wealth. It's possible. The itchy right ear (possibly the dominant one), the ear that detects sound that is put into words by the left brain's speech function, could have the capacity to react with an itch in preparation for an incoming pleasantry. The right eye when rubbed might, unknowingly energize the logistical left brain to become keen enough to identify something that it hadn't noticed before, something surprising.

Admittedly, these examples are simplistic and leave much to argue; but they are possible. In terms of universal correctness, it is unfortunate that the left side/right brain is always the negative "bad boy" in these sayings. Since the right brain controlling the left side of the body concerns itself with expressive and creative tasks, there is the possibility that during ancient times, when survival depended on generating material wealth, producing food, clothing, and shelter, the brain's expressive functions used in music, art, literature, and etc., were considered trivial uses that could only lead to negative results.

Science recognizes that the body (all matter) is surrounded by energy fields. Electronic measurements of these fields show that the body's right side holds stronger energies than the left.

The ancients used techniques that strove to balance these energies to maintain good health. Reiki is one of those existent modalities. The right-side energies are associated with assertiveness, determination, decisiveness while the left side has characteristics of nurturing, empathizing, fluidity, and coping. While both male and female hold these masculine/feminine energy fields, the right/male energies have come to be associated with strength while the female energies have been thought as being weak. It is clear to see that in those ancient periods of famine and wars, the masculine energies, whether dominant in males or females, were necessary to survive. This too could be another reason why these maxims laude the right side over the left. But ultimately, it is the story that it was the left side of God on which the devil sat before he was banished into hell that is the issue widely believed to have condemned the left side to the unlucky pejorative realm for all time.

THE BASES OF "SUPERSTITIONS"

Superstition is an interesting word. It comes from Latin *superstitio* "standing over in awe," or *superstes*, to outlive or to survive (newworldencyclopedia.org). A superstition stands above logic and reason. It is a belief that is not logical or reasonable to the norm of a society's thinking; yet, the belief does seem to live on and on. I often put the word *superstition* in quotation marks in this writing because the word often has an anti-Christian connotation. The proverbs and cures offered here by so many Italians might more accurately be called "folklore." Surely, at one time in history, some folks viewed these adages and remedies to be reasonable precepts, worthy to be handed down through generations, and reliably effectual as to be adopted into the folk culture. So, what caused these once reasonable ideas to eventually become known as illogical and unreasonable "superstitions"? How did they tumble down from folklore into the ignoble level of "superstitions?" The short and quick answer is Christianity.

In ancient times and in ancient civilizations there were no distinctions between animate and inanimate objects. All objects were thought to have souls (*anima* is the Latin word). All of nature was believed to have innate intelligence that positively acted on its own behalf. Roman and Greek gods were credited with creating and controlling all of nature and its environments. In the small communes and villages in Italy, the uneducated classes believed that the many disasters and evils that plagued the old and young alike, the calamities that happened without warning, were the works of offended gods and goddesses. Certain prayers, incantations, and certain rituals had to be performed to appease such gods.

Demeter, the goddess of agriculture could possibly be coaxed into encouraging robust crops by throwing grains of wheat, rice, or handfuls of flour onto the fields, or onto certain plow animals.

Jupiter, the Roman god of lightning and thunder might have been appeased by offering him a loaf of freshly baked bread as a distraction; or he might be assuaged by townsfolks banging on drums, or making loud noises to keep him away. These rituals are partially my own musings, but they are not far removed from the types that were actually performed.

Then came the Christian conquers and their missionaries. They saw these ideas and rituals as pagan behaviors not conforming to their catechismal teachings. They assumed ownership over the supernatural, declaring their Christian domain good and all others' demonic. They preached the belief in suffering and the idea that one should be resigned to hardships and not rely on magical ways to fend off misfortunes and malevolent forces. *There could be but one God who controls everyone and every part of nature* was their doctrine and they would dictate prescribed ways to worship Him and suffer His will. They denounced the ancients' beliefs as pagan superstitions and they forbade their practices. History records how Christians handled noncompliant peasants by condemning them to be burned at the stake, beheaded, crucified, imprisoned, or thrown into slavery. The peasants found a way around these injunctions, however. As Catholicism became the dominant Christian belief, the townsfolk began to ascribe their "superstitions" to the workings of saints instead of gods. Whereas the Roman goddess controlling lightning was Fulgora, the peasants prayed to Saint Barbara, designating her as the patron saint of lightning. The Greek god of animals and the wilderness, Actaeon, was turned into Saint Anthony (later St. Francis). And then followed, Saint Lucia protector of the eyes, Saint Anna, protector of pregnant women and babies, Saint Bologna protector of the teeth, and so on. By the time Italy and Sicily became one country, their people had knotted Christian, Mohammedan, Greek, and Roman beliefs into long ropes of Italian folkways never completely forgetting nor relinquishing their aboriginal ideas and customs. Out of their pagan practices they created a hybrid Catholic religion that pacified the Church; and in turn, the Church picked what battles they would fight, the local priests knowing full well that even with prohibitions these old-world ways would continue to be practiced, albeit in secret places. Here the Church condescended to allow their parishioners to keep a few superstitions and practices with the knowledge that eventually its populations would abandon old customs and come to follow the Church's full canonical laws

Fear is the catalyst for formulating these axioms and turning them into "superstitions." Since we can't be sure of the future and often are unable to explain what is happening at the present, we are inclined to apply our own meanings and attach our own fears to phenomena that science has not satisfactorily explained. Although most of us claim to be skeptical of these old-world beliefs, we still are reluctant to reject them completely. We fondly hold on to them and regard them like old photographs of departed loved ones called *Nonna, Nonno, Zio, Zia.* They are snapshots that evoke memories of cherished voices admonishing us to remove a hat indoors, cross ourselves when we drop a piece of bread, or take our elbow off the table. We avow that with all of our learning we are just too sophisticated to seriously give these adages any credence. They are curiosities of bygone days that we share while humoring their eccentricities. Yet, we share the precautions along with modern day Sicilians who, while looking over our shoulders, say, *Nun ci crirri, ma guardati.* "Don't believe any of it; but watch yourself."

To appreciate how these proverbs came about, it is helpful to know that in the early Italian environments of disease and poverty, communities and families turned to these aphorisms and trusted their efficacies out of necessity and in the absence of doctors, hospitals, and scientific studies. These axioms offered make-do remedies for injuries and health issues, norms for controlling families and protecting their environments. Households were apt to follow them for advice and peace of mind, holding more confidence in them than doctors, the confessionals, or the church.

The Italian immigrants to America, meaning North, South and Central America, carried little else than the clothes on their backs and these precepts and remedies. As they assimilated to the American ways, they blended their old-world beliefs with notions gleaned from the new world nationals, the latter class themselves immigrants and migrants. It is reasonable to assume that the "superstitions" handed down to us third and fourth generation, the ones recorded here, are a homogeny of American and Italian axioms. This collection, though far from being exhaustive, is offered here, unapologetically, doused with the parmigiana of Italian bias. Old country Italians passed along these adages to their progeny, those Facebook people who responded to my call and chose to generously share them with other readers. To reiterate an earlier point, somewhere and at some time in their experiences, our ancestors must have seen these "superstitions" work, or at least prudently heeded their cautions to experience positive outcomes. I think they are interesting features of our Italian culture, worthy of preserving, for as the writer John Aubrey (1626-1697) writes: *Old customs and old wives' fables are gross things, but yet ought not to be buried in Oblivione [sic]; there may be some truth and usefulnesse [sic] to be picked out of them, beside 'tis a pleasure to consider the Errours [sic] that enveloped former Ages: as also the present.*

— JOSEPH L. CACIBAUDA

INDEX

· ANGELS ·

The Scriptures support the belief that angels do exist. Matthew 18:10 quotes Jesus: "For I say unto you, that in heaven their angels do always behold the face of my Father which is in heaven." The teachings of the apostles make numerous references in the Scriptures that "compel the candid student of the Word to believe in the existence of angels" (Evans). According to the various writings in the Bible, angels are God-created beings, spiritual beings, and mighty and powerful beings. "Angels are not the spirits of the departed, nor are they glorified human beings" (Evans). "Originally all angels were created good" (Evans). Any talk of angels in these Italian proverbs almost always refers to the good angels rather than the fallen ones.

- *Don't misbehave at the dinner table or you will cause the angels to cry.*

- *Don't make ugly faces at the table or the angels might pass by and leave you like that.*

Guilt and shame are methods of behavior management. This admonition probably did work — at least for the short term. Other parents used fear to curb misbehavior around the dinner table. Ugly faces are certainly not helpful to the appetite; nor is their permanence a desirable prospect for the child's future.

THE SICILIAN LEGEND OF 101 ANGELS

RETOLD FROM A ST. JOSEPH ALTAR PAMPHLET *

A long time ago, a frail widow lived on the outskirts of a small village in Sicily. Her husband had died many years back and her children had left to work in the North. The widow was a devout soul attending church every morning and saying her rosary every night before going to bed. Living alone, her nights were often lonely and scary affairs. The wind would move things outside or cause something on the roof to creak and scrape, so that it sounded as though something or someone was trying to get into her small house. At these times, and there were many, she knelt next to her bed and repeated the prayer:

> ONE HUNDRED AND ONE ANGELS,
> WATCH OVER ME AND PROTECT ME,
> THOSE WHO COME TO DO ME HARM,
> DO NOT GIVE THEM STRENGTH
> OR THE FORCE TO OPEN MY DOOR.

The times in which the frail widow lived were hard times for her small Sicilian village; in fact, the whole area suffered poverty, with few jobs available. Poor people, to survive, often resorted to foul deeds they would never do under more opportune circumstances. Such was the predicament for a young man of the village. He was well aware that the frail widow lived alone and he reasoned that, living alone, she needed to spend little money. That meant that she surely should have an ample amount of cash stored some place. The young man thought that early morning might be a good time to pay her a visit because he knew she arose early to go to the 6:00 a.m. Mass. As he approached her house with the certainty that she would be gone, he saw a number of people working in her yard and coming out of and going into her door. He abandoned his mission and thought it would be better to visit her in the early afternoon reasoning that this was the time for *riposo*, the daily nap; and, remembering that old people sleep soundly, he could sneak in and make off with her money before she awoke. The next day, he waited until 1:00 p.m. to go to the frail old lady's house. Again, there were people painting her fence, raking her yard, trimming the shrubs. The only thing left to do now was to wait until late night and break into her house. If she awoke during his burglary then he'd have to decide what to do next.

So then, around midnight, the young man slinked around the deserted streets heading toward the old lady's house. He carried an ax for the door and a rope for the old lady. As he reached her door, certain that no one saw him, he laid the ax on the ground to inspect the lock to see how he might break it open. He saw that it was very rudimentary and fragile and that one small whack would do the job. He put down the rope and reached over to pick up the ax, but to his surprise, it would not budge. It had become so heavy that he couldn't move it an inch. Panicking, he thought of taking his rope and perhaps pulling open a window to get in, but the rope became as heavy as an anvil. Not only was he unable to budge the rope or the ax, he began to notice that his legs were getting wobbly and he was having trouble standing. Stricken with fear and bewilderment, the young man ran away as fast as his shaky legs would take him.

It was 2:00 p.m. the next day when the young man woke up to a dazzling sun streaming through his window. He couldn't be sure that he hadn't dreamed of his trying to get into the old lady's house. There would be a good way to find out. He'd go to her house to see whether his rope and ax were still there. As he approached her small house, the frail old lady was standing just outside her fence watering a shrub. "Good afternoon, *Signora*," he said, "I was passing by your house late in the evening when I dropped my ax and my rope. Have you seen them?"

The little lady moved aside and sure enough laying right where he had set them down were his rope and his ax.

"Ah yes. Well, thank you, my good Signora," he said and bent over to pick them up with no trouble at all. As the young man started to leave, he turned to the old lady and said, "I noticed you had a lot of people working in your yard a couple of times I passed by. Where did all of those people come from?" The widow smiled, but did not answer because she knew immediately that the young man had intended to do her harm.

Those "people" he saw had been parts of her nightly prayer. They were the one hundred and one angels watching over and protecting her.

* St. Anselm Catholic Church, Madisonville, Louisiana

• AUGUST/MAY •

- *It is unlucky to marry in August or May.*

There are a few cautions that involve the months of August and May. The ancient writer Ovid speaks of a Roman festival called Lemuria that took place in May and lasted for three days, and sought to appease the restless departed souls. These restless souls were of the murdered ones. The festivals took place during the rule of Augustus, thus May, the actual month, and August, the name-sake month of Augustus, were considered to be unlucky and morose months, especially for such joyful occasions as weddings. June became a popular month for weddings because it was the first acceptable month after May. There is perhaps another explanation for the months' poor reputations. It is not that August and May are unlucky months, but on the contrary, they are auspicious months, both dedicated to the Immaculate Heart of Mary. The Church set aside May to honor Mary; and, each day of the month included a daily practice honoring Her. A wedding held on a day in May, aside from being difficult to schedule with the Church, would have interfered, even competed, with a sacred day of religious practices, risking the displeasure of the Holy Mother. Since August too was filled with as many days of dedication, the same explanation might have applied to August weddings.

It appears that there was a standing rule that maids could not marry on a festive day, as many of them were captured and forced to marry. The belief being that the brides would weep bitterly on these festive days dedicated to the gods, which would cause the gods to dole out bad luck to the marriage (Plutarch).

- *It is unlucky to buy a broom in August or May.*

To buy a broom in such holy months of May and August dedicated to the Holy Mother might have been interpreted as giving too much consideration to such an implement, one associated with witches and sorcery. Homes were usually adorned with holy pictures and sacred objects, more so during these months. Bringing a new broom into that consecrated setting would have been seen as disrespectful, improper, and unlucky.

- *Don't sweep away spider webs in August.*

The Bible treats spiders and spider webs in positive and negative ways. The web is often used as a symbol for sin's snare. In some places, spiders are viewed as positive creatures of great works and wise for their small size. The spider's web is also seen as a symbol of God's protection, a shield that traps all harm. There are the stories of cobwebs hiding the baby Jesus from Herod's soldiers, and spider webs concealing Mohammed and St. Felix as they were hunted by their enemies. Since the broom is usually associated with witches' spells, it is possible that sweeping away webs considered, in the Biblical sense, protective things, should be avoided.

Also, there is a folklore that reads the shapes of spider webs to prognose weather and other coming conditions. The Farmers' Almanac says that large webs are signs of a cold winter to come. Thin, frail spider webs predict dry weather. A spider web that quickly dries from dew means a "fine day." Spiders moving down from their web predict a rain. "Spiderwebs [sic] floating at autumn sunset: bring a night frost, on this you may bet."

The Almanac lists August as the best month to harvest vegetables, so perhaps destroying spider webs in that month, which according to Google Search is the optimum month for spiders to spin webs to mate, might have something to do with unnecessarily removing useful predictors. It is interesting to note that some early cultures mixed spider webs with oils to cure sores. It could be that refraining from sweeping away spider webs in August, their peak months, was a way of having an ample supply on hand for these uses.

· ANIMALS ·

- *It is a bad omen when you see a dead bird on your path.*

- *Birds at one's window foretell a death.*

Birds are suspicious creatures because they are free to move from earth to the sky, which some associate life to death, earth to heaven. Angels are depicted with wings and they are often associated with coming from and going to the other side. We are apt to think of a bird flying against our window, or into our house as a disguised angel coming as a messenger of death, or coming to search for a new candidate to usher away.

Regarding the "dead bird on your path": Considering we may subconsciously associate angels with birds, then certainly having a dead angel in our path would be a terrible omen.

Additionally, birds were observed by the ancients to be able to forecast changes in the weather, and to have phenomenal homing instincts. These instincts were seen as powers to predict coming events. The events depended on the type of bird. A black one, the raven and the crow for examples, always forecasted coming sorrow — death.

- *A dog howling means there is an impending death.*

Romans believed animals had supernatural powers. It was written that a howling dog preceded Caesar's death. Believers thought that their howls could cast spells and summon the ghosts of dogs from hell. The goddess Hecate's arrival was announced by howling dogs. Hecate was the goddess of death and a sorcerous.

- *If you take a picture of your animal, the animal will die.*

There is the belief by some people that the camera captures not only one's image, but one's soul with the shot. It would seem here that animal souls might be more vulnerable to capture than human souls. The belief is that once their soul is captured, surely the animal's death soon follows.

- *If a bee or spider should get on you, put your tongue to the left side of your mouth and they won't bite you.* (See ***MOUTH***)

· BABIES ·

- *Don't go to a funeral or a wake if you are nursing a baby. It will turn the mother's milk sour.*

Anything that affects the mother might naturally affect the quality of her breast milk, if not causing it to sour, at least passing along some of the mother's emotions through breast feeding. Funerals evoke sad and macabre low energies which could affect a mother's milk. Articles on the topic state that stress can affect breastfeeding in a couple of ways: the supply of milk and the content of the milk. The body releases hormones that deal with emotional situations that can indeed impact the mother's health. The adage above uses the term "sour" whereas current studies use the word "cortisol," a hormone that regulates emotion. An emotional mother secretes an abundance of cortisol, which is then ingested by the baby, making the child easily agitated in unfamiliar situations.

Also, pregnant mothers were always told to stay away from things and situations that might frighten them for fear that the developing embryo might be negatively affected. It is well known that whatever the mother is exposed to, the baby is exposed to. Funerals would be one of those frightful events that mothers should avoid. (See *Pregnancy*)

- *Overstating that a baby is beautiful may incur the wrath of the evil eye, unless you say "God Bless" after complimenting the child.*

The premise here is that the devil is always interested in beautiful babies and children. If you compliment a baby without saying the right words "God Bless," you are exposing the child to the devil. In the same sense, the evil eye is often spurred to wrath by jealousy. Excessive compliments of a baby would unnecessarily bring the child to the attention of a jealous one who would be so envious of you for having such a beautiful baby, that he or she might cast an evil spell on you or the baby, or both.

- *Tape a quarter over a new-born baby's belly button to keep it from protruding.*

Perhaps the sheer weight of the quarter held tight by tape would help keep the navel from poking out. At any rate, it seems to be a reasonable and inexpensive means of managing the belly button's height and appearance. At least one will always know where to find a quarter.

- *Garlic pinned to a baby's shirt will keep away evil spirits.*

In ancient Greece, garlic was served to Hecate, the goddess of the dead. Hecate taught witchcraft and sorcery. Through this association, garlic has become closely associated with the world of the occult, including death. It would seem in this case that the garlic should actually attract the goddess of death and evil spirits rather than repel them. Perhaps then the garlic is to appease the evil spirits if they do show up. Rather than chasing them away, it might distract them so that they forget about the baby and indulge themselves with the garlic. However, in addition to stopping bed wetting, curing tooth aches, lowering blood pressures, garlic continues to be used as a means of keeping mean spirits, including vampires, at bay.

- *Don't stand at the head of a baby in the crib or it will be a simpleton.*

The child in the crib is a developing form and as such, it is easily influenced by its environment.

In yogic lore it is written that energy enters (and exits) the body through the top of the head. The hair acts as antennae to capture surrounding energies (See *Hair*). Newborn babies have two openings on their head called fontanelles. One is at the back of the head and the other is at the top of the head. These eventually close as the child grows. This could be a basis for such a warning. Consequently, it might be wise to steer daffy Zia Pina or Ziu Cicciu away from your child's head; and so, to be extra safe, you should keep everybody clear of that location.

- *Non family members should always kiss Babies on the feet, never on the head or face to protect the child from being spell cast with a "Judas kiss."*

We all are aware of Judas and his betrayal of Christ with a kiss. In the realm of Italian beliefs, the family should constantly be alert to dangers from the outside, particularly concerning their babies, the most vulnerable members of the family; non-family members pose certain risks since the family may not know them well, or, simply because they are not family. Then too, considering how Judas marked Jesus for the Romans, the belief is that a stranger may so mark a child for the evil eye with a kiss. Kissing the feet shows subservience, never control. The gesture to a new baby indicates humility and the lack of an ulterior motive. Additionally, there is always the issue of health where illnesses are more apt to be transmitted from the face, the nose and mouth areas, than around the feet.

- *It is good to give sugar as a gift when a baby girl is born and you first visit her home.*

A popular nursery rhyme dating from the early 19th century declares:

> WHAT ARE LITTLE BOYS MADE OF?
> SNIPS, SNAILS
> AND PUPPY-DOGS' TAILS
> THAT'S WHAT LITTLE BOYS ARE MADE OF

WHAT ARE LITTLE GIRLS MADE OF?
SUGAR AND SPICE
AND EVERYTHING NICE
THAT'S WHAT LITTLE GIRLS ARE MADE OF

There is a source in a Google search for "sugar in ancient times" that reports that sugar was a valued and expensive spice during ancient Rome because it had to be imported across the Indian Ocean. I doubt whether the above prescript goes back that far. It seems more to be in keeping with the nursery rhyme above. At any rate, something sweet is always a welcomed gift.

- *Don't take a baby outdoors until it is christened.*

There is always a danger that something terrible could happen to an unbaptized baby, worst of all death. According to early Catholic doctrine, a child that died before being baptized was considered pagan and went to a dark realm. In later Church doctrine, an unbaptized child goes to an ethereal realm called *limbo* (*limbus infantum*), a place of waiting for the soul, a place of indeterminate salvation for the child. The bible does not directly mention this level, but it is written of in Dante's Inferno. Catholic doctrine says that the baptized child receives the blessing and protections of the Saints, and should the worst happen before christening, he or she will go directly to Heaven.

- *Plant a fig tree on the north corner of the house when you bring the first-born home.*

As regards the north direction let us remember that many of our sayings have roots in pagan beliefs. The word "pagan" shouldn't automatically discredit the premise of the saying. These early people based their ideas on observations and experiential results. We know scientifically that

the rotation of the earth creates a magnetic field that has to impact what happens at various locations and directions of the planet. Each cardinal direction has its own magnetism that is beneficial to achieve certain ends through rituals, spells, creating weather patterns, affecting agriculture, etc. The cardinal direction of the NORTH is known to astrologers as the Earth element. According to them, the Earth element represents the feminine principal of the Universe; the Mother Goddess from which all life comes and returns. The Mother Goddess represents fertility, nurturing, and respect for the earth. One of the goddesses of the Earth element is Demeter, the Greek goddess of agriculture. As I have often written, Italians rarely plant anything that does not yield a fruit, a nut, or a vegetable. What better tribute to a newly born child than dedicating a sturdy fruit bearing fig tree placed in the Northern part of a yard, the Earth Mother's own place?

• *Don't let a baby look into a mirror for a year.* (See **MIRRORS**)

• BLESSED MOTHER •
• LA BEDDA MATRI •
• LA BELLA MADRE •

- *Children were often told that their misbehaviors cause the Blessed Mother to cry.*

One contributor said that she was always doing something to cause the Blessed Mother to cry. *Pòvira picciotta. Pòvira la Bedda Matri.* (Poor young girl. Poor Blessed Mother.)

- *A loaf of bread placed upside down on the table causes Blessed Mother to cry. (See **BREAD**)*

• BLESSINGS •

- *Make the sign of the cross whenever you pass a Catholic church.*

- *Make the sign of the cross when you hear a siren.*

- *Make the sign of the cross with oil to cure a stomach ache.*

- *Make the sign of the cross and then kiss your fingertips if something frightens you.*

- *Use pictures of Jesus or the saints to calm a storm.*

- *Throw out blessed Good Friday palms during a storm.*

- *When someone sneezes, say "God Bless You." Italians say "Salute."*

- *Wear a blessed scapula from your church and a holy pin on your clothes for protection and health.*

- *Put a scapular between your mattresses to keep you safe at night.*

- *If you see a hearse go by you must cross yourself or you will be next.* (See **DEATH**)

- *Bless the house with holy water, especially a new house.* (See **HOUSE**)

- *After a wake or funeral, you must go home and cross your doorway before going to someone else's home or you will carry bad luck with you.* (See **DOORS**)

The ultimate way to receive blessings for a Catholic is to form the sign of the cross. The custom dates back to at least the first century after Christ's birth. A standardized technique was formulized 300 years later. It is interesting to note that the original movements involved the thumb, forefinger and middle finger all touching, In India these hand gestures are called *mudras*. They control energy flows in the body. To Catholics they represented the Holy Trinity. The three fingers touched the forehead, the heart, the right shoulder and then the left shoulder. Pope Innocent III (1198-1216) allowed the sign to be altered to touching the forehead, the heart, left shoulder and then the right shoulder as a replication of returning from misery (left side is again seen as negative) to crossing over to glory (right side is the hero) in the symbolic recognition that Christ triumphantly crossed over from death to life.

Making the sign as one passes a church signifies that at that particular moment that person is reminded of Christ and asks his blessings. Making the sign as one hears a siren means that at that particular time he or she is sending prayers to Christ to protect all of the people involved. Making the sign of the cross over one's stomach or any other part of the body signifies that at that moment that person is asking for a healing from Christ, just as the priest makes the sign through the air to ask for a blessing for his congregants.

Anthony DeBlasi remembers, "The Sicilian well of supplication to Jesus, Mary, Joseph and the saints, was filled deep with words of comfort for every distress. My childhood headaches had all been soothed away with a special prayer and a gentle massaging movement of mother's thumb over the center of my forehead, imitating in miniature the sign of the cross."

Silent thought-prayers create subtle vibrations, sound waves. "Sound waves are waves of pressure." These "waves of pressure" can influence healing just as light waves can affect healing. (Levy)

As regarding pictures, statues, medals, scapulars, prayers, and incantations (affirmations), I offer this idea to readers in the spirit of science more so than the nature of a sermon.

We know that physics tells us that all of matter, what we know as our physical world, is the result of molecules vibrating at different rates. The forms of matter preserve individual properties because their molecules vibrate at given speeds. All matter is perpetually vibrating, either as light waves or as light particles. The subject of a picture retains its distinctive features of shapes and colors, which is its identification, due to the reflection and absorption of light waves that strike it, but also due to the rate of vibration of the light particles that create the shapes and forms of the medium on which it rests. Pictures of saints, whether they are painted, drawn, or photographed, must contain the unique arrangements of light vibrations of the saints lest they would not portray their likeness. These light vibrations/images must convey to the devotee the inherent qualities of the subject; in the case of saints, their holiness. It follows that our thoughts and our utterances are vibrations; and their energies, pressure waves, continue forever through the atmosphere and through space. Once spoken, words cannot be retained or regained. Spoken prayers are words that seek to attune their vibrations with the natural vibrations that nurture and balance the universe. It is through this attunement that desirable results, blessings, occur. These blessings are experienced as answered prayers. (Luke12:32 "It is your Father's good pleasure to give you the kingdom.")

On the other hand, malevolent and malicious speech (curses and spells called *fatturi* in Sicilian) produce vibrations that are at odds with the natural vibrations of the universe and they create disturbances in the atmosphere that cause upheavals, like physical disasters and social unrest. (Proverbs 15:1- A soft answer turneth away wrath; but grievous words stir up anger.")

Sacred relics and statues, prayers, positive thoughts, chanting, positive affirmations, cherished pictures of loved ones by the very nature of their blessedness, all vibrate in tune with the universal flow of atoms, and so they do positively affect our vibrating-matter-bodies and vibrating thought-wave minds—and they do favorably impact our matter-rife world and thought-filled environment. It is not the chalk or brass of a statue or the quality of paint on the canvas that evokes the sacred ambience one feels in a place of prayer, but markedly, it is the vibrations in the likenesses of the icons and the lingering vibrations of spoken and thoughtful words of prayers that linger in the environs.

You need not have any religious beliefs for blessings and prayers to work, although a believer is apt to recognize and appreciate their effects more than an agnostic. You need not believe in gravity to have it work on you, but some appreciation of its power certainly will dictate how far down you can safely jump.

It is worthy to note that in some Italian communities, the faithful Italians were not very forgiving of saints to whom they fervently prayed and made offerings if the saints denied their supplications. They threw rocks at the saints' likenesses, and called them awful names, sometimes painting, vandalizing, or burying their statues. A prayerful wish may not always be forthcoming. The subtle meanings and reasons for unanswered prayers are understood sooner, later, or never, according to the devotee's faith, and particularly their understanding, which is made keener by recognizing the physics of blessings.

BLESSINGS FOR SNEEZERS

Just about every culture has an affirmation to recognize when someone sneezes. Each culture offers a different response followed by some reply. Most cultures use words that mean health, but there are others, like English speakers who offer words of blessings. There are almost as many theories to the origin of blessing one who sneezes as there are responses. Some claimed the heart stopped during a sneeze, so a quick response was needed in case the beating didn't resume. Others write that people thought the soul was expelled with a sneeze leaving the body as in death. A blessing or statement of good health quickly recovered it. Ancient people believed sneezes were deathly omens or warnings from the gods, especially during the times of the plagues; and then others feared that a sneeze allowed evil spirits to enter the body, and that by blessing the sneezer the evil spirits were held at bay. This is what Aristotle (384-322 bce) says about sneezing: "Why do men sneeze? That the expulsive virtue and power of the sight should thereby be purged, and the brain also from superfluities; because, as the lungs are purged by coughing, so is the sight and brain by sneezing; and therefore, physicians give sneezing medicaments to purge the brain; and thus it is, such sick persons as cannot sneeze, die quickly, because it is a sign their brain is wholly stuffed with evil humors [earth elements], which cannot be purged."

— ANONYMOUS

· BREAD ·

- A loaf of bread placed upside down on the table causes Blessed Mother to cry.

- Make a cross in the flour before you begin making bread.

- One should never lean on a table while making bread. It shows disrespect to Jesus.

- It is not good for the housewife to drink water while kneading the bread; lest the dough will cool, the leavening will be compromised resulting in terrible loaves.

- If you drop a piece of bread, make the sign of the cross before you pick it up. If the piece was their own, they kissed it after picking it up.

- The correct way to serve bread is to break the loaf, not cut it.

- Bread from St. Joseph's altar can be thrown outside to calm a storm.

Italians take their bread seriously. It is a rarity to have an Italian meal without bread on the table.

In the poverty plagued villages of Italy, bread was often the only food to eat. Stories abound about farmers and miners eating only bread and onions each day for lunch. I suspect that it was always served with meals as filler because there was little food to eat for the main course. Since bread has always been an Italian mainstay, it is exalted in the culture and considered sacred. Then there its role as the Christian symbol of Christ. The old Italians believed that if you mishandled bread, you mistreated the body of Christ. Loaves must always be set upright on a table, to turn a loaf upside down was to place Christ face down, thereby showing disrespect. To these Italians from the old country there was no difference between a piece of bread and the sacramental host. It was sinful to disrespect either one.

In some parts of Italy, cutting bread was once considered sacrilegious, seen as re-wounding Christ's body. This is why one had to "break bread," a gentler way to apportion out a loaf. However, as time went on, the Italian way of holding the loaf against the chest and cutting it with the knife toward you became the accepted respectful technique.

IN REGARD TO ST. JOSEPH DAY BREAD:

The bread from a St. Joseph Altar has been blessed by a priest so it is consecrated. From ancient times, Romans believed that holy bread had the ability to calm storms. St. Peter chased away mad dogs by giving them blessed bread. The host thrown in a river caused demons that ran along its surface to sink. Devotees living in the southern parts of the country experience yearly hurricanes and so they store St. Joseph's Day bread to use in storms. There are many Catholics in the South of Italy that will strongly avow it works.

· BROOMS ·

- *Never take a broom from your old house to your new one.*

It is posited that an old broom having dealt with all of the unwanted debris and energies from the old house will carry those negative entities into the new. It stands to reason that a new broom will bring in new desirable energy into a new house, provided you do not buy one in May or August.

- *It is unlucky to buy a broom in August. Some say May.* (See ***AUGUST/MAY***)

- *If you suspect an evil entity is near, place a broom upside down at your door so the evil thing will spend the night counting every straw and not have time to enter.*

- *If a neighbor curses you, put out a broom, a braid of garlic, or a chili pepper. The curse will be sent back to them.*

Here the broom no doubt symbolizes the instrument that will sweep the curse back in the neighbor's direction. The plait of garlic perhaps comes from classic Greece where garlic was a favorite dinner for Hecate, the goddess of the dead. Since Hecate taught witchcraft and sorcery, garlic became associated with the world of the occult. The red chili pepper is a charm that will keep away the evil eye. (See ***MALOCCHIO***)

- *If you sweep the feet of a single person, they will never get married.*

Here the sweep necessitates a broom, an instrument considered to be of witches and sorcery. But, after all, the broom is an instrument for cleaning dirt and refuse. Its many bristles ensnare the negative entities, particularly if the entities are psychical. Here it is believed these evil elements may be dislodged by passing the broom over one's feet. The feet symbolize one's foundation and one's connection to the earth. They support us in our attitudes, our endeavors, and in our relationships. Humans' mobility and positions are actuated by their feet. A broom sweeping across such a symbol of one's foundation could put a spell on that person to prevent those feet from walking down the matrimonial aisle. It is interesting to note that the term, "Swept off their feet" suggests the opposite of this old adage. That is, one that is swept off their feet (bedazzled by another) is more a candidate for marriage than not.

- *If a broom accidentally touches another person while one is sweeping, he or she must spit on the bristles to keep from bringing bad luck to the person touched.*

Many charms involve spitting, like spitting on one's hands for good luck, spitting on a pair of dice, spitting on money, spitting on your hands to begin a strenuous task. It seems that saliva is another way to bless something. Mothers use their spittle to rub away a child's hurt arm or leg, the saliva being curative because it is uniquely the mother's. Spitting on a broom's bristles counteracts bad luck by using the unique and unduplicatable spittle of an individual. Because of its one-of-a-kind properties it chases away evil agencies. (See **MALOCCHIO**)

In Sicily, a propitious time to sweep under the bed and in the corners of each room is the Saturday before Easter Sunday. Mops and sticks may also be used to chase away the devil while chanting: *"Fuora Diavolo. Trasi Maria"*— Get out Devil. Come in Mary

The fact that a broom sweeps away dust and debris indicates that it has the capacity to sweep away any other unwanted entities. There is a notion that the handle and the bristles of a broom could possibly resemble the *Tree of Life*, an impactful symbol in Ancient Europe. In pagan Europe the *Tree of Life* also represented the connection to one's family and to one's ancestors, the bristles representing the many connections to the members. This broom-to-tree relationship might have something to do with some of the origins of the warnings about when to buy one and which way to stand it during certain situations. Of course, there is the connection to witches that gives the broom the negative qualities of bringing bad luck. It was believed that evil spirits that liked to hide in bushes were able to get inside the home and hide within the broom's bristles. In pagan cultures, winds were thought to be created by the witches' brooms. The broom shaft doubled as a magic wand.

- *Sweep out of the front door of a new house to get rid of any evil spirits.* (See *HOUSE*.)

- *Don't sweep the floor on New Year's Day or someone might leave the house forever.* (See *NEW YEAR'S DAY*)

THE AMBITIOUS BROOM
FROM A STORY BY E.T. CORBETT (1830-1899)

Once upon a time, a broom stood in the corner of a little shop. It was waiting anxiously to be bought. May went by and no one dared buy a new broom then since May was one of the unlucky months to buy one. June passed and everyone celebrated weddings, never thinking of buying a broom. July passed quickly leading into August, where the town folks held fast to the belief that August was also a bad time to buy a broom. The sad little broom waited patiently. September and October went by and in November, the little broom was delighted to see the owner approach and lift it from the corner; but he only moved it into another corner.

December came around and it was just before Christmas, when the shop owner brought in a number of Christmas trees standing them in the corner from which the little broom had been removed. But there was one tree that did not fit and so the shopkeeper moved it next to the little broom. The Christmas tree, its leaves smelling of cedar, stood with its green branches overshadowing the little broom; it looked down condescendingly at this plain long stick atop a pedestal of gathered straw.

"I will soon be dressed in ribbons, adorned with candles and fancy strings of popcorn, and I'll stand over candies and lovely presents. Everyone will gather around me admiringly and I'll be the center of attention until January sixth," the tree boasted.

Of course, the broom could not compete with that glorious scenario. It knew what its future held.

Very soon, a gentleman and a poorly dressed woman came into the store. The man, examining all of the trees, decided to buy the tree that stood next to the broom. The poor woman walked around the store unmindful of anything or anybody, slowly chose a scrubbing brush, then a bar of soap, and finally, as an afterthought, she took hold of the broom.

All that day and the next, the broom was kept busy sweeping the house until it became very tired and weary. The poor woman's three children stood ready to help by moving chairs and tables aside so the mother could sweep in their places. They all knew they were getting ready for Christmas.

"But where is our tree?" asked the children. "Can't we have a tree?"

The poor woman bowed her head and said, "Dear children. We are too poor to buy a tree this year. I spent the last bit of money on this broom.

"I wish that ugly broom was a Christmas tree," said the oldest child, a girl named Lisa.

"I wish I was a Christmas tree too," thought the broom.

"Let us make a tree of the broom," the eight-year-old girl named Minnie said.

"How?" asked Lisa.

Minnie ran to the corner of the kitchen and snatched up the broom She took it into a small bedroom and tied it to the back of a chair with it bristles up. Then the children began hanging ribbons, and colored paper, small China figurines, a pop-corn ball, and whatever trinkets they could find. The poor woman, seeing what her children had done, gave them a bunch of pink and red flowers she took from an old hat she no longer wore. The children were delighted with their results and sang and danced around the decorated broom.

The broom was very happy and grateful that its wish had been fulfilled.

Come Christmas Eve night, as the children slept, the mother hung upon the broom some sticks of candy, fruit, and homemade cookies. In the morning, the children were delighted to see what presents their mom had given and they spent the morning playing around the broom/tree. The broom stood with pride.

One thing was missing. The broom/tree lacked lights. So little Johnny, the one boy in the family, went to a neighbor's house and got a few small candles. The children delighted in placing them on the broom/tree. The decorations were now complete and the broom stood emblazoned in the soft light of the candles, its ornaments vivified all the more in the light.

Now, the little family, pleased with their ingenuity, sat down to have their Christmas dinner, leaving the broom in the next room.

Suddenly, Lisa jumped up and yelled, "Our tree. Our tree. It's on fire!"

It was true. The candles set the colored paper ablaze, which then caused the red and pink flowers to burn, setting off some of their dolls and trinkets as well; then, the broom's bristles began to burn.

The poor woman quickly doused out the flames with a bucket of water, but not before the broom was completely destroyed, its bristles completely incinerated.

"My new broom is no more," said the woman.

"Our tree and our decorations are all gone," cried the children.

They were all sad; but not the broom. The broom was pleased at how things turned out. It had gotten to be the center of attention and it had gotten to have a day of rest and—just as the Christmas tree would be thrown out, the little broom too would be discarded and never have to sweep and clean again.

· CHILDREN ·

- *Don't walk around in your socks, you will stunt your growth.*

This admonishment presumably applies to children who are developing day by day. It is in the class of warnings about drinking coffee, smoking cigarettes, not eating vegetables, and eating too much sugar. The experts aver that poor health is one cause for stunted growth and obviously smoking cigarettes, drinking lots of coffee, an inadequate diet, would impact the health of a growing child. Another cause of abnormal growth is too little exercise. At the risk of taxing the readers' limits of indulging my explanations, it could be that the "walking in socks" might be an indication of the child staying inside; and, in staying too much inside, he/she might be apt to have too little exercise. Or, it could just be a means of scaring a child enough to stop dirtying their socks or wearing them out by walking in them inside or outside.

• COLORS •

- *Red Ribbon in a new car keeps evil away.*

Red is believed to be the color of energy, strength, power, passion, and fortune. It also stands for love of God and God's love of man, thus it is the color used to ward off the evil eye. Red is also used to indicate anger and revolution. Red roses show love. Turn red with anger. (See **INTRODUCTION**)

Green has many associations, such as vegetation, life, jealousy, and money. It is the symbol of living things, rebirth, and regeneration. Green palms are used during Easter season and people "turn green" with envy.

Blue is associated with calmness and spirituality. The Church made it the symbol of faith. The Virgin Mary is usually associated with blue to show her celestial nature. From ancient times, blue was the color of truth and wisdom, hence the expressions "the blue heavens" and "true blue person."

Yellow denotes brightness, cheerfulness, but it can also can mean sickliness and death; and of course, meekness or cowardliness. In the Middle Ages, sickness and personality traits were attributed to the condition of gall, the yellowish bile in the gallbladder. A spiteful, malicious person was thought to produce more bile than the normal person. A sneaky, cowardly person was also considered to have unhealthy gall. When discovered, sneaks and cowards were forced to wear yellow hats or cloaks. A coward is considered to be yellow, while yellow flowers brighten up a room.

Black in most cultures intimates evil, ignorance, and death. In the dark, there is an ignorance of everything around us, which produces fear. In other cultures, the color represents the soil of the earth, which supports fertility. Black is the total absence of light, which makes it antithetical to the 272 Biblical passages that extol light. Black absorbs all colors of the spectrum, which subliminally suggests that it swallows up, it annihilates, making it scary. The Romans, dating back to 753 BCE, wore a dark toga while mourning, and that custom was carried into Italian use, and widows wore black. Romans also wore black to protest unpopular laws. The fear of black or absence of light brought to the popular expression "scared of their own shadow."

White has traditionally represented divinity, purity, and limitlessness. The color white reflects all the colors (the wavelengths) of the light spectrum. This characteristic has the implications of openness and magnanimity as well as intimating unlimited possibilities. Popular adages are "as pure as the driven snow" and "little white lie;" the last one implies that the lie was not that serious and as a matter of fact the motive behind the lie was to promote a positive end.

• DAYS •

- *Don't start a journey on a Tuesday.*

- *Don't marry on a Tuesday.*

Some of the possible reasons for Tuesday being unlucky are:
  - Tuesday is thought to be an unlucky day because it is the day Christ was tortured.
  - The Greeks considered it unlucky because it was dominated by Ares, the Greek god of war.

- The Romans considered it unlucky because Tuesday in Latin is *martis,* named after Mars, the Roman god of war.
- Constantinople is believed to have fallen on a Tuesday during a Crusade and then the Turks overran the city 200 years later on a Tuesday.

Mondays are unlucky because it was the day Cain was born; the day Abel was slain; the day Sodom and Gomorrah was destroyed; and the day Judas was born.

Many of these good/bad labels were works of astrologists who ascribed their influences according to positions of heavenly bodies and the effects they wielded on one another. Of course, most countrymen were unable to plan their lives around propitious and risky days and concluded that any day is a good day for a good and honorable person.

- *Don't not clean or sweep on Ash Wednesday.*

The ashes used on Ash Wednesday are usually from the burned palm branches from the previous year's Palm Sunday Service. The prayer given as the ashes are placed on the forehead include the passage, "Remind me that I am but dust." The prayer reminds the devotee that he/she should use the time they once spent on whatever-it-is-that-they-choose-to-give-up-for-lent to pray and reflect. Sweeping would suggest spending time on a menial task and a symbolic rejection of dust, the object represented by ashes, rather than reflecting purely on the message of Christ.

(See also ***FRIDAY/GOOD FRIDAY***)

- *Don't wash clothes on New Year's Day or there will be a funeral.* (See ***HOUSE***)

- *Change sheets on Saturday.* (See ***HOUSE***)

THE LUCKY DAYS

Giovanni Francesco (c 1485-1558)

Once there lived in Cesena, in Romagna, a poor widow named Luc-ietta. She unfortunately had an only son named Lucilio whose stupidity and laziness had no equal. He would lie in bed till noon, then get up to take a nap in a hammock. He would get up from the hammock, grab a bite to eat on the way back to his bed to rest. In short, he was the clearest pic-ture of the greatest sluggard on earth. His grieved mother every day hoped that he would someday become the support of her old age; and she never ceased to urge and advise him to be more active and industrious.

"My son," she often said to him, "he who would see good days in this world must exert himself, be industrious, and rise at break of day; for lucky days favors the industrious and the vigilant, but never comes to the lazy and sluggardly. Therefore, my son, if you will believe my counsel, and follow it, then you shall see good days, and all will fall out to your heart's content."

Lucilio unquestionably heard what his mother said, but, not be-ing the brightest candle in the chandelier, he did not understand the meaning of her words. His mother's talk had interrupted his bed to hammock routine and, to humor her, he sauntered out of the house to walk along the road before the city gate. The short walk exhausted him so he stretched himself out in order to take a nap right across the path-way, so that all entering or leaving the city could not avoid stumbling over him.

It so happened that the very night before, three men of the city had accidentally discovered a buried treasure. They had waited for day break to dig it up and were carrying it home, when they came upon Lucilio, who still lay across the road, no longer sleeping, but only looking up at the sky with his hands as a pillow for his head.

"Heaven has sent you a good day, friend," said the first of the three men, as he walked over him.

"Heaven be praised!" said Lucilio, when he heard the words. "Now I shall have a good day!"

The man with the buried treasure thought that Lucilio somehow knew what he and his friends had been up to and the "good day" Lucilio alluded to meant sharing the treasure.

The second man then stumbled over Lucilio, likewise wishing him a good day. Whereupon Lucilio, still dwelling on the good days, said, "Now I'll have a double share!"

The third followed and saluted him as the two others had done, also wishing that Heaven might send him a good day.

Lucilio sat up and clapped his hands exclaiming, "Oh! delightful! Now I have got all three of them! I am fortunate!"

Lucilio's three lucky days referred to the good days the men wished him, but the men in their paranoia though he was talking about the treasure. They feared that if they didn't share it with him, he might go to the authorities to tell of them and their treasure. So, they took him aside and told him the whole affair. Of course, Lucilio, not being the sharpest arrow in the quiver, didn't understand in the least what the men were confessing to him.

Well pleased with getting his lucky days and a sack full of money, Lucilio carried the treasure home to his mother, and said, "Dear mother, Heaven's blessing has been with me; for, as I did as you desired, I was vigilant enough to be given good days. Take this money, and buy with it all we require."

His mother was very confused since Lucilio's explanation made no sense to her, but throwing her hand in the air in the attitude of "what's the use?" she welcomed the money and urged him to continue doing what he just did to get more lucky days.

• DEATH •

• *If you see a hearse go by you must cross yourself or you will be next.*

The sign of the cross protects Catholics from many evils, principally death. The sight of a hearse reminds one of their own mortality. The Sign is made as a token of thanks that one is alive and well enough to see the hearse go by. It is customary for a funeral procession to move along very slowly. The idea of the pace is to display the solemnity of the motorcade; but its slow pace tradition is a carry-over from the days when the processioners all carried candles and had to walk slowly to insure they would stay lit (Panati).

• *Hold on to a button if you see a hearse go by.*

A button is a mundane object, part of the worldly plane. It is usually round, the circle being a symbol for many things: the earth, the sun, the moon, and the seasons. Some cultures use the circle for protections. Holding on to a button, a circular object, helps anchor one to the earth while affirming that earth is where they wish to stay long after the hearse goes by.

- *No hats on a bed or a death will occur.*

This could have its origin from the occasions when a priest or a doctor entered a home to administer help to a sick and/or dying person and naturally put his hat on the bed when he arrived. That image would conjure the fear of bad luck and death.

- *Dreaming of back teeth falling out means you will learn of a death.*

Dreams of teeth falling out are common. One idea is that the loss of something in a dream means the loss of someone in one's life. Usually, these types of dreams are brought about from worry and stress. Also hearing about a death or suffering might precipitate these types of dreams. Artemidorus (200 AD) was specific about whose deaths one might learn about when they dream of teeth falling out. He wrote that the upper teeth represent the demise of important people in the household while the lower teeth represent less important ones.

- *Birds at one's window foretell a death.* (See ***ANIMALS***)

- *Cover all mirrors after a death.* (See ***MIRRORS***)

DISH TOWEL

- *Dropping a dish towel on the floor after dark means dirty people will come visit you.*

As pagans believed everything in the universe was interconnected, and all objects had souls, this saying perhaps is based on the concept that there are no insignificant, non-consequential actions; that all events signify some meaning. The dropped dish towel itself is an undesirable event that may also be seen as careless. The floor, dark, and dirty people are all rather unpleasant elements associated with dropping the dish towel, its own state of cleanliness notwithstanding. My conjecture here is that one's carelessness with the dish towel would result in the penance of an unwelcomed visit from dirty people.

· DOORS ·
· & CHARMS ·

- *After a wake or funeral, you must go home and cross your doorway before going to someone else's home or you will carry bad luck with you.*

- *Don't stand in an open doorway.*

- *Always leave a house from the same door in which you entered it.*

- *Enter and leave the house with the right foot (See **RIGHT VS LEFT**)*

We are apt to be misled by these doorway prohibitions. It is not the doorway that affects the good or bad luck, but the threshold, "a strip of wood, metal, or stone forming the bottom of a doorway and crossed in entering a house or room" (Oxford). Some sources state that the threshold was designed as a barrier to keep seed that was separated from the grain, principally wheat, called thresh, from coming out of the storage structure. Other etymologists write that "thresh" means to stamp, beat, thrash, suggesting that one had to stamp or thrash their footwear on the threshold to clean them before entering the building. It is not known where the "hold" part of the word came from in this latter definition, perhaps to hold what material was shaken from the footwear. Nevertheless, the word threshold has come to mean crossing over into a different place.

Door charms are affixed above and along doorways to prevent any evil entities from crossing the threshold. In the American Journal of Philology, 1911, M.B. Ogle wrote an article about doors in Greek and Roman Religion and their folk-lore. He writes: "...the most prominent belief in connection with [the threshold and the door] was that spirits haunted the vicinity." He furthers quotes Pythagoras who says that "If you stumble upon the threshold on going out, you should turn back." The reasoning here is probably this: the stumble foretells of coming bad luck unresolved by passing over the threshold. Going back over the threshold and passing under the charms, should clear off the negativity. The chance that the bride might stumble on the threshold is the bases of the groom carrying her over it. Here it is reasoned that a bride's stumble would be an inauspicious way to begin a marriage, and a presage of other mishaps in coming times.

Ogle goes on to write, "[Among the Greeks and Romans] the threshold, or the vicinity of the door, was the place for performing all sorts of magic rites, which are, in the last analysis, generally concerned with the spirits of the dead." Our Italian associations with magic and death, good luck and bad luck, have their origins in ancient Roman and Greek cultures.

- *Palm fronds from Good Friday placed above the door frame keep evil spirits from entering the house.*

From ancient times, palm branches were the symbols of goodness and victory. Palm Sunday commemorates Christ entering Jerusalem when palms were placed in front of him in his path.

The palm also is a sign of eternal life.

- *Orange peel placed over door way brings good luck.*

- *Ram's horns or other horns place on the door frame ward off the evil eye.* (See **MALOCCHIO**)

Oranges are connected with sunlight and are considered lucky fruit. As cited above, Ogle's journal article refers to a vast number of charms the Greeks and Romans used on their doorways and under their thresholds. Plants, bats, frogs, horns and the like were fastened by nails to a house's doors to keep away evil spirits. The nail was as important as the objects it held because of the positive earth element energy in metals. Ancient rulers drove nails into the temple walls to get the attention of the deities whenever they wished to end scourges. Additionally, doorways were smeared with pitch, fox blood, wolf's fat for further protections. While our modern amulets are perhaps not as bizarre in the scope of "things" hung or smeared over and around doors, their histories begin with these early amulets.

- *Sweep money out of your door then back into your door three times to insure you always have money.* (See **MONEY**)

• DREAMS •

• Dreaming of back teeth falling out means
you will hear of a death. (See **DEATH**)

• Dreaming of a death means
you will hear of a birth.

• Dreaming of a birth means
you will hear of a death.

There are astrologers that aver dreams of death are hints of a change, a new birth of circumstances. Perhaps the birth mentioned above is hearing of the birth of a new opportunity, or the challenge of starting a new job, or project, or a new life journey; and, quite possibly, news of a new baby.

Regarding the dream of a birth: The origin of this saying could come from a couple of underlying beliefs. It could be derived from the belief that every new birth has to have a corresponding new death, the idea that a dying star symbolizes a new birth. Or, the saying could reflect the essential fatalism so often espoused in Italian literature and familial stories that indicate that even when all is well (the joyful birth of a baby) this doesn't guarantee that all will end well (a death).

· DRINKING ·
· & EATING ·

- *Don't drink cold water before or after eating a banana. The banana will turn into a solid ball in your stomach.*

According to steptohealth.com "Drinking cold water after eating can cause indigestion because the cold temperature changes the consistency of the foods we've eaten. This makes them harder to digest "

- *Don't eat while standing or your feet will grow big.*

This sounds like something *Nonna* would say to her *niputi* to keep them at the table longer. It infers that all of the food eaten will drop down and there the nutrients will act on the feet to unduly cause them to grow faster than the rest of the body. This is an example of a saying that was blithely spoken to a child by parents or grandparents, one that will always echo, if lucky, in one's ears in the voices and with the inflections of their dear ones. Remembering fondly their hand gestures, body movements, and facial expressions that added emphasis to the sentiment, these cautions hold special places in the lives of those of us who were fortunate enough to have heard them firsthand. This one and the "socks" warning (See **CHILDREN**) are not to be taken literally or pondered over seriously, but only understood as another subdued way these great ones showed their love.

FIG TREES

- *A bone break from falling out of a fig tree will never heal.*

The fig tree should be the official tree of Italy, or at least share it with the olive tree. The Romans highly regarded the fig tree believing its leaves shaded the infant twins Romulus and Remus and its branches helped to keep their basket upright as they floated down the Tiber River. It remains highly regarded by Italians. It could be supposed that one climbing in a fig tree is in a sense mistreating it, and he/she is justly punished and left unhealed by the disrespect. Then there is the tree's disrepute at the hands of Jesus in Mathew 21 where Christ was hungry and came upon a fig tree that was bare, so he cursed it. This may be the source of the thinking that one falling out of a cursed tree will not ever heal his bones. It must be said, however, that no Italian would ever think of a fig tree as an evil creation of nature, nor would they purposely shinny up one.

- *Plant a fig tree on the north corner of the house when you bring the first-born home.* (See **BABIES**)

THE FIG TREE

Leonardo Da Vinci (1452-1519)

There was once a fig tree that produced no fruit. Because it was barren, no one would look at it. In spring it grew large healthy leaves, but in the summer, when other trees bore fruit, the fig tree had none to offer.

51

"No one notices me. If I grew big luscious figs, people would stop to look at me," sighed the fig tree.

It wished and prayed and prayed and wished that it could bare figs. Finally, one summer, the sun seemed to favor the tree so that figs grew and grew; and the larger they got, the sweeter they tasted.

Now everyone passing the tree took great notice of it. They had never smelled such fragrant figs nor seen such a large fruit. Soon people were snatching at the fruit, violently shaking the tree's branches, striking it with long poles, and climbing through it so that its branches eventually snapped off. When the day was done, the poor fig tree was bent and broken, its leaves were torn, and many of its beautiful figs lay on the ground crushed under foot. Once again, the tree stood there bereft of fruit.

Moral: Those who cry for attention may soon find, to their sorrow, that they receive more than they want.

· FRIDAY ·
· GOOD FRIDAY ·

Adam and Eve are said to have fallen from grace on Friday. Also, Christ died on the cross on Friday. Friday nights were associated with the nights witches got together to plan their mischief.

- *Don't wear new clothes on Friday.*

There is a reply on *www.sites.psu.edu* called "Why You Shouldn't Wear New Clothes on a Tuesday." The writer's mom wore new dresses on consecutive weeks and each dress met with a mishap on each Tuesday. She then remembered the East Indian advice. Since Friday is considered an unlucky day by many Westerners, the no-new dress on Friday warning would apply. A Sicilian belief found in a manuscript in the Palermo library says, "…whoever cuts out garments on Tuesday or a Friday runs the risk of making them too short and of losing the cloth. Such clothing has little wear in it for nothing begun on these days has any durability." (Law-Rence).

- *Friday is an unlucky day to sail.*

Perhaps because Friday is named after the goddess Freyja, the goddess of witchcraft and death, many consider the day to be unlucky. Freyja's number is 13, which is considered an unlucky number. Freyja's day is Friday the 13th. Coincidentally, Freyja's father is Njord, the sea god which might have something to do with sailor's not wanting to sail on that day.

There is a Welsh tradition that says water-sprites keep a watchful eye over the seas on Fridays, and this causes the seas to be tempestuous and dangerous. There is an old sailors' legend of a ship setting sail on a Friday morning carrying a young man and a beautiful maiden. Their good looks were seen as supernatural. The vessel never reached its destination, but on certain nights a phantom ship can be seen just off shore bathed in an ethereal light; and standing on its deck, the two lovers (Law-Rence).

- *Don't wash clothes on Good Friday.*

In some parts of the world, countrymen believe that a local saint visits houses every Friday and if she sees sewing, spinning, and washing going on she damns the women as sinners and causes sicknesses, sore eyes, hair and fingernail losses. To the passionate believer, Good Friday was a sacred day, like Sunday, where menial work was supposed to be substituted with prayers. With Mondays traditionally set aside for washing, one who washes clothes on this sacred Friday would seem to be demeaning the day.

Fridays are auspicious days in Sicily, not unlucky days. There is an Italian belief that whoever is born on Friday will be of sanguine temperament, passionate, light-hearted, and handsome. They will be musical, fashionable, and will talk a lot. They will be immune to the evil eye.

Women in Sicily kept chicken eggs laid on Good Friday for luck and protection from bodily harm. Even today Good Friday eggs are either served as meals or used in baking Easter breads.

In Palermo, women would go to the graves of loved ones on Good Friday to ask if the departed ones' wishes had been fulfilled over the year.

- *Plant basil and parsley on Good Friday.*

- *Do not dig up the ground on Good Friday.*

Up until the 60's as I recall, Good Friday was a day the family did not play a radio, watch television, go shopping, visit others, eat meat, or work in the garden. It was a day of quiet reflection to acknowledge the sacred gravity of Christ's death. These two gardening admonitions seem to conflict, probably owing to their locales. It would seem the latter advice would be more in keeping with the quiet motif of Good Friday. As for the first suggestion, the Farmer's Almanac does praise the advantages of a Good Friday plantings.

- *Throw out blessed Good Friday palms during a storm.*
  (See **BLESSINGS**)

- *Palm fronds from Good Friday placed above the door frame keep evil spirits from entering the house.* (See **DOORS**)

- Cover all mirrors on Good Friday. (See **MIRRORS**)

• HAIR •

- *Cut your hair when the moon is full and it will grow faster.*

There seems to be some disagreements between hair stylists and astrologers as to the best time to cut one's hair. The website www.beauty. onehowto.com agrees with the above recommendation. It says, "The full moon is the perfect phase to undergo a considerable haircut ... To have a haircut during full moon encourages it to grow with more health, abundance, brightness, and strength." Astrologers and hair stylists claim that the pulling affect the moon has on the earth acts on our bodies, particularly our hair. While stylists admit there is no scientific basis for this idea, many claim good results with cutting hair according to the phases.

- *Snip a piece of hair at the beginning of March to keep from having headaches.*

There is an Irish belief, reasonably believed adopted by Italians, that snippets of hair can be used to carry away ailments. One method was to place the hair clips on a bush so that animals, primarily birds, might carry them away, one hoped, along with the illness. The saying, "Cured by the hair of the dog that bit you," might come from this belief. The *malocchio* believers claim that the evil eye can use hair clippings and also nail clippings to attack one. As regards the headaches, March tends to be a month of seasonal changes. Accordingly, healthcare specialists claim that these changes bring on allergies, sinusitis, and even stress. It is possible that the old timers expounding this aphorism wisely snipped some locks to set aside at least until they got past the Ides of March and the hangovers of St. Patrick's.

- *If you drop a comb, step on it before you pick it up.*

The superstition is that if one drops a comb, then a disappointment will follow. Throughout history, hair has always been an important component of the human body. Hair is the subject of legends and superstitions everywhere in the world. There is an old Sicilian belief that some children are born with special locks of hair that insure they always have protection from all harm and good luck. If parents were to cut these locks, the child would incur God's displeasure and the child would develop poor eye sight, or spinal weakness, or even a crooked neck. One's hair is the first identifier we see, its color, its length, its coiffure; and, we immediately form impressions by what we see. Samson's hair was the source of his strength, as indeed it is believed in some practices that hair captures a certain amount of energy prevalent in the atmosphere and brings it into the body. In the early Christian times combing priests' hair was a special part of the preparations for religious ceremonies. Some religious historians even ascribed mystical qualities to the comb. This saying must reason that dropping one's comb causes its mystical powers to be temporarily disturbed. Added to this, the energy in the hair that is caught in the comb might leave one more vulnerable to receiving bad energies of disappointments when the comb is dropped on the floor. From an energetic point of view, stepping on the fallen comb, grounds the implement, taking from it any of the unwanted energy that allowed it to be dropped in the first place.

- *Do not go outside with wet hair lest you get a cold.*

This maxim is not medically true (mayoclinichealthsystem.org). It is probably based on the idea that the cold season is the season of colds and flu which equates to one getting cold and thereby catching a cold. Chances are that one will catch a cold in cold weather because they tend to spend more time indoors, possibly around others who might be infected with a cold. However, there is an underlying element of nurturing within this warning, a mother, aunt, or grandmother's advice, easily construed as overprotective, nevertheless, well-meaning and loving. It is one more way of telling their loved ones to be careful. "My grandmother used to think that one would die if they ventured out with wet hair," writes Mark Hehl. He and his siblings were forbidden to venture outside with wet hair.

- *Be careful who cuts your hair lest they keep locks of your hair for evil purposes.*

It was believed that evil entities would use a person's hair, fingernails, or teeth to put on wax dolls, or straw dolls, or embed these items in fruits or vegetables as models of the person they wished to curse. They then would drive nails or pins in sections of the effigy to invoke pain and suffering. There are stories of families that consistently encountered hard luck until they discovered what some later called "spite dolls" under their steps or hidden in other spots around the house. (See *EVIL EYE*)

- *Grandfather knew what crop of hair to pull to relieve headaches, colds, fevers.* (See **HEALING**)

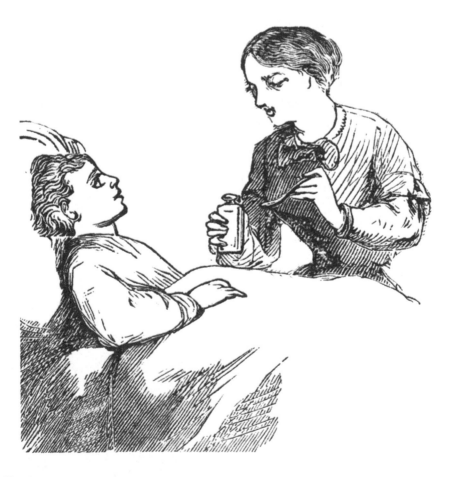

• HEALING •
• TECHNIQUES •

CUPPING:

Richard Gambino described this procedure in his book, *Blood of My Blood*:

"An empty cup like receptacle was turned upside down and a match lighted within it, the match held in place by a homemade device. The inverted cup with its burning match was placed on the afflicted part of the person's body... As the flame consumed the oxygen in the cup the pressure in it would be reduced creating a suction which would pull the patient's flesh into the cup. The point was to have the cup draw the sickness out of the body."

Of course, small drinking glasses, *i bicchierati*, were also used in the same way which formed large red circles on the skin that would eventually fade into the skin's original color. The idea of sucking out the malady was very much akin to placing leeches on the body to draw out impurities.

— Anthony DeBlasi

• *Grandfather knew what crop of hair to pull to relieve headaches, colds, fevers.*

Chances are Grandfather stimulated an acupuncture point in the scalp. Acupuncture pictures shows a site on the back of the head, at the level of the top of the ears where this location relieves tension headaches. There are other area of the body that can relieve colds and fevers. There are spots to rub on the hands, feet, forearms, elbows that alleviate colds and fevers. I recall my father showing these exact locations when he talked about getting rid of colds and fevers, and even headaches. To help with headaches, the scalp is massaged first to get it ready for the pulls. You begin with the front of the head and work back grabbing a small crop of hair between the thumb and forefinger. The tufts of hair are gently pulled "until you hear a sound as if you were pulling something apart," (like cracking one's knuckles). The process is continued until you've covered the entire scalp; or, as the article says, "You can choose particular places to pull according to where the pain is concentrated" (Marveli).

- *Rub injuries with olive oil.*

Oleic acid is the main fatty acid in olive oil. It is said that this acid can reduce inflammation in the body by reducing levels of C-Reactive proteins. Good olive oil can lessen the pain and swelling in arthritis. Grandparents' and parent's touches added a powerful factor to remedy injuries and ailments; and, yes, the olive oil helped.

Sicilian affirmation "cut the worm" was said while rubbing the stomach with olive oil, then saying a prayer to get rid of worms.

In the time this precept was offered, the health conditions in Sicily were such that tape worms were endemic. Besides rubbing the stomach with the oil, no doubt the oil was also ingested. It is claimed by health proponents that taking olive oil every day for a few weeks can rid the gut of bacteria. The affirmation and the prayer while rubbing were added comforters.

Ettore Grillo writes an account of "cut the worm" in his book, *A Hidden Sicilian History: Second Edition*:

> "[Aunt Filippa] then asked me to lift my T-shirt and bare my belly. Finally, she made certain arcane signs on my stomach and at the same time said a special secret prayer in a low voice, which she repeated three times. Since I was a cu-

rious boy by nature, with very fine hearing and an excellent memory, I heard and imprinted in my mind the secret prayer to cut roundworms, which I now disclose both in the original Sicilian and in English:

RAZZIONI PPI TAGLIARI I VIRMI

TAGLIU LI VIRMI NE STU CURPU
TAGLIU UTTU E TAGLIU NOVI.
TAGLIU LI VIRMI NE STU CORI.
LUNI SANTU, MARTI SANTU,
MIRCURI SANTU, IUVI SANTU,
VENNIRI SANTU, SABBATU SANTU
A DUMINICA DI PASQUA.
MORI LU VERMI E 'N TERRA CADI.

PRAYER TO CUT ROUNDWORMS

CUT THE ROUNDWORMS IN THIS BODY
I CUT EIGHT AND I CUT NINE.
I CUT THE ROUNDWORMS IN THIS HEART.
HOLY MONDAY, HOLY TUESDAY,
HOLY WEDNESDAY HOLY THURSDAY,
GOOD FRIDAY, HOLY SATURDAY,
EASTER SUNDAY.
THE ROUNDWORM DIES AND FALLS ONTO THE FLOOR.

When her prayer was over, she recommended I drink a small glass of olive oil with squeezed lemon and raw mashed garlic, the following day in the early morning.

I followed her instructions, and I have to say that I actually excreted a lot of roundworms.

Some of them were dead and some looked dazed." (p.55)

- *Rub injuries with coal oil.*

Maggie J. Hall writes, "Historically, individuals have used coal oil, also called erroneously in the past as kerosene, as an antiseptic, decongestant, and as a pesticide. The substance was readily available and less expensive than a conventional visit to the local physician." Coal oil is refined petroleum extracted from a type of soft, oily coal called cannel coal. This type of coal results from the slow decomposition of woody fiber plants and the tissues of insects and other animals over many years. Apparently, these combinations aid healing of many skin conditions and other injuries. One must be cautious however to sit away from a fireplace once treated.

- *Use lemons or oranges to draw out poisons from a wound like a nail puncture.*

There are studies that show that citrus fruit, especially the peels, produce antimicrobial compounds that could be essential for microbial infection resistance (Sass).

- *Use tobacco for a bee sting.*

In a treatise called *A History of the Medicinal Use of Tobacco 1492-1860*, GG Stewart identifies tobacco as an agent for successful uses on "Bites of poisonous reptiles and insects; hysteria; pain, neuralgia, laryngeal spasms; gout, improved growth of hair, tetanus... wounds;..." It is not smoked, but moistened to form a clump and applied directly to the sting. In olden times it was chewed to moisten, and then applied, the spittle having some healing agents in itself.

- *Use cow manure for a bee sting.*

Cow manure is still used by many African tribes to manage burns and other wounds. Only recently, in 2019, have researchers begun to study the components of cow dung that make these age-old remedies successful. Although research is still going on to identify the sources of the healing agents in the dung, biologists suppose the digestive enzymes that aid the cows with the ingested plant-proteins are part of the source, along with perhaps the actions of the microorganisms that feed on the cow dung. As these researchers breakdown the small chemical elements in these enzymes they discover that they are also found in known healing substances (Gololo).

- *Irish potato slices put in a scarf and held at your forehead will be draw out a fever.*

- *A raw potato over a sty will cure it.*

- *Remove a wart by rubbing it with a potato and then burying the potato during a full moon.*

From *Off the Grid News*: "Potatoes have many constituents including a host of tannins, flavonoids, and alkaloids. The tannins have a drying action, which has been linked to relieving diarrhea. They have also been used externally for burns and inflammation. In folk medicine, the use of potatoes for bone and muscle pain is partially due to their ability to hold heat for long periods of time, allowing it to penetrate deep into one's tissues. The converse is also true, as they hold cold well and are also used as a compress for treating burns and scalding. The alkaline properties of potato juice have an antiseptic action ..."

It appears that "burying the potato during a full moon" might have more benefit for the potato than the wart.

   •   *An onion put in a stocking and held under your arm or under your foot will draw out fever.*

The website *Healthy and Natural World* features the article: "Onions on Feet or In Socks for Flu, Colds, Detox, and Infections-Does It Work?" It sources the Journal of Traditional and Complementary Medicine as saying that there is anecdotal evidence of the positive effects of reflexology on health conditions. Reflexology uses certain energy points on the feet, hands, and other body parts to address certain health conditions that affect corresponding body organs. Onions are said to draw out infections and toxins, so placing them in stockings or under one's arms have been found to be effective in relieving fevers and detoxing the body, at least anecdotally, if not scientifically. There are other Italian suggestions that garlic be used in the same way, that is, on the bottom of one's foot.

- *Boil bay leaves to cure a baby's colic.*

"Another amazing feature about bay leaves is its ability to clear up your respiratory system. If you have a cold or a nasty cough, bay leaf can help unclog stuffy air passages and get rid of bacteria. Boil 4–5 bay leaves in water. Once it's cooled slightly, soak a washcloth in the bay leaf water and apply it on your chest. Make sure the cloth isn't extremely hot before applying it anywhere on your body" (curejoy.com).

- *Rub stems of artichokes to get rid of warts.*

Artichokes are rich in vitamin C, vitamin A, iron, potassium and antioxidants. They also contain flavonoids, which studies show act as a chemotherapeutic agent that arrests cell growths and aids in cell deaths. These studies show that vegetables like artichokes are rich in flavonoids and have the potential for controlling tumor growth (Choi).

- *A grandmother used her wedding ring brought around the eye to cure a sty and also to cure ring worm.*

In some branches of holistic health, usually based on ancient Eastern beliefs, metals have the capacity to draw in, neutralize, or expel energies emitted by the planets. There are other energies on earth however that can affect the body with fear, stress, anxiety, and depression, to name a few. Copper, gold, silver and iron metals are used in these healing modalities to balance the energy levels of the body. Bringing these metals in contact with human tissue can affect them at their cellular levels to bring about cures. Chances are Grandmother's ring was one of these metals and that she didn't know anything about these Eastern beliefs, but was using a technique handed down through many, many generations.

• HOUSE •
• MAKING •

- *Change sheets on Saturday.*

Monday used to be laundry day and since Friday was not a good day to begin a task, it looks like Saturday was the best day for this chore. Or perhaps to keep from doing any work on Sunday, one should change the sheets on Saturday for Monday's washing. There is also the idea Saturday, the day before the day of the Lord, is a day for good thoughts and shedding negative energies gathered all week. Changing the bedding at the end of the week might have been one of the ways to throw off negativities so that one wakes up on Sunday with positive attitudes.

- *No shoes on the counter, table, or on a chair.*

There are many societies that expect visitors to take off shoes when they enter the home.

Shoes are apt to pick up and carry with them filth and of course, the energies of areas through which they traveled. Aside from being unsanitary, one shows a high level of disrespect by putting such a base and unclean object on these surfaces where food is served and families gather and sit.

- *Always return a kitchen vessel with something in it even if it is a piece of candy.*

This is a common courtesy on the level of sending one a thank you note for a gift. There is no threat of bad luck, or promise of good luck for doing this, only a show of proper etiquette.

- *Bless the house with holy water, especially a new house.*

Catholics have the parish priest bless a new house. Water is one of the energy elements. The others are earth, wind, and fire. Water is considered a feminine energy because of its nurturing qualities like cleansing, healing, purification, life sustaining. The priest adds a fortifying quality to it with his blessings.

- *Don't wash clothes on New Year's Day or there will be a funeral.*

According to some beliefs, washing clothes on New Year's Day denotes the washing away of someone near and dear. This goes along with the idea that if one chooses to wash on that particular day they risk washing away all of their good luck for the rest of the year.

- *Three people should never make a bed together because it is bad luck for the youngest one.*

In the Middle Ages "making a bed" was a literal term. The bed was made of sacks filled with straw. With the lack of heat in the buildings it was not unheard of nor lasciviousness for many people, including guests, to sleep in the same bed to keep warm. In the morning, the hay was removed from the sacks to be used in other ways and everyone helped with "unmaking the bed." At night the hay was placed back into the sacks, that is, the people helped "make the bed" (Panati).

While this bit of history is interesting it is more likely that this proverb is derived from the fact that it is difficult enough for two people to agree on anything, but in terms of making a bed and whose bed is being made there could possibly be problems with three people even maneuvering around a bed without getting in one another's way. The bed is a rather personal territory and unless two or three sleep in it, as in days of old, the one owner will surely have his/her idea on the standards of how it should be made. Bearing the preceding in mind, one can understand how another version of this axiom, "only one person should ever make a bed. If two people make the bed there will be a quarrel," is not such a far-fetched statement. Another rather extreme maxim adds that if three make the bed, the third person will die. Usually, three is a lucky number associated with the Father, Son, and Holy Spirit; third time is a charm; three wise men; land, sea, and air make up the earth. On the other hand, three can represent negative events: three strikes and you're out in baseball; bad things happen in threes, including deaths; Jesus told Peter he would deny him three times before the rooster crowed. Then there is the wartime scenario where the third man to light his cigarette on the same match would be killed. The reason being that by then the enemy would have seen the match-light and zeroed in on their target. This warning about making the bed probably has something to do with deaths happening in threes.

- *Sweep out of the front door of a new house to get rid of any evil spirits.*

The peasant Sicilians were careful when they swept out the house. As they constantly called in angels to protect them from evil spirits, they would welcome in three. One angel stood at the door, one sat at the table, and the other watched over the bed. Any sweeping had to be done before the evening because that is when the angels stood guard over them and the house. To sweep out anything at night would risk sweeping refuse in the face of the angel at the door.

It would seem that a new house would not have accumulated evil spirits so soon, but perhaps the above axiom tells one just to be safe, sweep out evil spirits out of the front door; and, do the sweeping with a new broom. Of course, there are other proverbs that warn us not to sweep dust out of the front door because along with the dust one sweeps out good luck.

- *When you move into a house, put potatoes in the corner of each room to encourage good spirits to stay.*

Potatoes have many nutritional and medicinal uses. It is possible that the many positive uses by some cultures would suggest to them the idea of placing them around the room to attract good spirits. Italians have many plants and foods, including the potato, that have helped them stave off starvations and illnesses.

- *Don't stand in an open doorway.* (See **DOORS**)
- *Always leave a house from the same door in which you entered it.* (See **DOORS**)
- *Enter and leave the house with the right foot.* (See **DOORS**)

· KNIVES ·

· AND OTHER ·
· UTENSILS ·

- *The giver of knives must be given a silver coin in return to keep the friendship. And they must say:*

"IF YOU LOVE ME, AS I LOVE YOU
NO KNIFE CAN CUT OUR LOVE IN TWO"

It is reasonable to suppose that knives were usually considered tools of combat. In early Greece, the knife was the weapon of choice for duels. The coin along with the affirmation would have been given to make clear the friendly nature of the gift.

- *Do not cross utensils, knives, spoons, or forks on the kitchen table. It is bad luck.*

The thought here is that crossed objects conjure up the image of the crucifixion, which of course symbolizes a bad ending. Another belief is that crossed utensils will cause an argument, the crossed knives resembling crossed swords, the ritual action to indicate a challenge to combat.

The gesture of crossing objects creates hindrances to any of the objects to move in its intended way. This impediment would most certainly create arguments. On the other hand, earlier in Italy, in the 16th

century, there was a model of decorum where a diner crossed the utensils in the plates to signal that one had finished the meal and to make a show of thanksgiving for the food by consciously forming a cross (Panati).

- *If you drop a spoon, a woman is coming to visit.*

- *If you drop a fork, a man is coming to visit.*

- *If you drop a knife, a whole family is coming to visit.*

Here is a purely imaginative explanation for these three beliefs. Early pictures of upturned spoons show that they were ornately decorated to resemble the upper torso of a woman and the lower spoon part, a woman's bustle. The upturned fork, once only two tines, resembles the male figure. The later three tined forks still brought to mind a male figure, albeit with the male's middle appendage. The knife can be said to be an amalgam of the two; that is, its lower part narrows the bustle and closes the tines to produce a solid combination of both—the family. None of the above explanations are founded in any source; they are, as stated, purely imaginative.

There are some sources that say that the fork was once a symbol of luxury when most people stabbed at their food with the sharp end of a knife, or picked it up with their hands. Women were the first to use forks as the men viewed

them as signs of effeminateness. Spoons, on
the other hand, did have fancy handles, usually shaped in the likenesses of the saints
and were used by the very wealthy. It became a custom to present a newborn with
a silver spoon adorned with saints to bring
good fortune to the child. Thus, the term,
"Born with a silver spoon in his/her mouth"
(Panati).

- *Cut a string with a knife to calm
  a storm.*

Cutting the apron strings is a term used to
mean "lessening the extent to which someone controls, influences, or monitors someone else" (Farlex
Dictionary of Idioms, 2015). It is stated in other
places (Collins COBUILD Idioms Dictionary, 3rd
ed, 2012), "Verbs such as loosen or let go of can be
used instead of cut." Perhaps the intent here is to let
go of the fear of the storm by cutting the string, thus
calming the effects of the storm. There is also the
term of "a string of bad luck" which might have to
do with a string of bad storms. Additionally, there
are legends that tell of sea witches tying knots in
ropes (maybe strings), each knot was believed to
have the energy to cause and to stop different
types of winds, including hurricanes (Cowie).
Separating the string from the knots by cutting
them would have calmed a storm.

- *Do not give knives as a wedding present.*
  (See **WEDDINGS**)

· LAUGHTER ·

· *If you laugh too hard, then you will have to cry as hard.*

There are a few proverbs that express this sentiment. The Giuseppe Pitre fable below deals with this sentiment somewhat. My book *After Laughing Comes Crying* (*prima arridi a poi chiangi*) is taken from the proverb, "He who laughs when he is young cries when he's old." There is another one, French, that says, "He who laughs on Friday cries on Sunday." And then there is, "If a person sings before breakfast, he will cry before supper." All of these express the idea that too much high spirits bring on evil consequences. This sentiment has formed the Italian and particularly the Sicilian ethos that exhibits, so says Pirandello, "an instinctive fear of life," and a fatalistic view of the future. On a more practical level, these proverbs also mean that one who does not plan for the future and spends his/her time in over indulgences is doomed to future hard times and sadness.

IN THIS WORLD ONE WEEPS AND ANOTHER LAUGHS.

GIUSEPPE PITRE (1841-1916)

Once the Lord, while he was making the world, called one of the apostles and told him to look and see what the people were doing.

The apostle looked and said, "How curious! The people are weeping."

The Lord answered, "It is not the world yet."

The next day he bade the apostle look again and see what the people were doing.

The apostle looked and said, "How curious! The people are laughing."

The Lord answered, "It is not the world yet."

The third day he made him look again. The apostle looked out and said, "This is very, very curious. Some of the people are weeping and some are laughing."

Then the Lord said, "Now it is the world, because in this world, one weeps and another laughs."

· MALOCCHIO ·
· EVIL EYE ·
· DEVIL ·

- *Be nice to certain relatives or they might give you the evil eye.*

A curse or a cast spell is called *la fattura*.

All cultures have an evil eye. The underlying cause of someone casting an evil eye is jealousy. In this respect, one should not intimidate relatives to the point of making them envious or jealous.

- *Red Ribbon in a new car keeps evil away.* (Also See **COLORS**)

According to the ancient cultures, all of the mishaps that did befall man were the results of the evil eye. Most prominently, diseases and sicknesses were considered to be works of demons, and so they were treated by priests, not physicians. St. Augustine wrote, "All diseases of Christians are to be ascribed to these demons..." Needless to say this attitude of the Church stymied medical progress for centuries. As time went on the countrymen, unsatisfied with mere words from the clergy, demanded concrete means of personally asking God's favor. Here the church offered objects of veneration, sacred clothes, crosses, thorns from the crown, pieces of wood from the cross, scapulars, etc. People began using charms, talismans, rituals, incantations, and the like to expel the influences of the evil eye. These early charms had to be sufficiently odious to drive out the devil—livers of toads, blood of rats, parts of executed criminals. The newer charms and talismans were easier to procure and their efficiencies were based on their natural properties often defined by astrologist. Earth, wind, fire, and water were considered to be the elements that influence nature. If they influenced nature, they nullified the evil eye's powers. So salt, for example, was used as an earth substance to keep away the evil eye, thus keep away bad health and bad luck.

The evil eye, *malocchio*, or *iettatura*, has existed all over the world from time immemorial. The belief has outlived the reigns of conquering nations, the dogma of various creeds, and the influence of the Christian church. Some still quietly consider it to impact their lives today although most dismissively call it a superstition. In spite of glibly calling it a superstition, those that approach the belief do so as the Sicilians say "Nun ci crirri, ma guardati." *Don't believe any of it; but watch yourself.* The concept of someone being able to bewitch another always creates a fascination. In fact, the word fascination, *affascinare*, is the word for "bewitch." This bewitching is thought to be done by an evil eye, the *malocchio*, a malicious force that is precipitated by envy, or jealousy. Ancient philosophers warned that infants and young animals were more susceptible than other life to the negative influences of the evil eye. In these pagan times, women were believed to have more evil eye powers than men, which was perhaps the genesis of witches and their sorcery. Fortunately, countrymen weren't helpless against the malevolent forces of the evil eye; there were remedies. Mothers that suspected the dark presence carried around wolf tails, rue cuttings, onions, different colored plaited scarfs, cloves of garlic, to name a few talismans. There were certain chants, prayers and rituals in which these articles were used to escape the powers of the eve.

In many various ways and customs, the evil eye has been and still is at the heart of people's "ever-present dread of ill omens." Thus, the events of a black cat crossing in front of a person, one dropping a certain object, entering and exiting from the same door, making decisions and performing certain activities on a Friday, hearing a dog howl, a rooster crow, seeing a bird at the window, and others, are signs we still try to avoid and pay attention to them when they occur. Since the incendiary element that inflames the evil eye is envy, or jealousy, persons in many countries will not accept a compliment without giving the praise to God. Thus, to the compliment: "Oh you have never looked better today." an Italian will say, "Grazie a Dio." The Irishman would say, "Glory be to God." The English farmer might say, "Lord be wi'us."

As the uneducated peasants became more and more guarded against the evil influences of the *malocchio*, they began to fear the presence of it in their deities and God's representatives on earth—the saints. They began to fear that punishments for their sins would not just be visited on them, but on their families. Here the Christian church furnished the people with empowering means to neutralize retributions from the gods and saints. The Catholic church offered the confessional, the body-of-Christ host, the crucifix, the sign of the cross gestures, the candles, the incense, the altar, holy water, the rosary, certain prayers, sainted scapulars, to name a few. In contradistinction to the Church's sacred amulets, secular icons like purposely obscene amulets and bodily gestures were used to ward off the evil eye. The *mano fico*, for example, was a hand sign directed toward the evil eye where the thumb was held between the index and the middle finger. This is the equivalent to the extended middle finger sign and it means the same thing. The object of these amulets were supposed to show one's power to shock, confront, and insult the evil eye with offensive gestures. Necklaces were, and still are, worn with this hand shape as well as phallus talismans. Their shocking natures were used in the same way as the horrid, grisly masks one sees on Oriental temples and the hideous gargoyles found on large cathedrals over the world that are intended to confront and scare off evil forces.

CORNU

The most efficacious sign that neutralizes the evil eye's powers is the bull's horn, which resembles the crescent moon. The Roman goddess Diana was associated with the cult of the moon and she also was known as the goddess of childbirth. Diana's embodiments carried over to the Madonna in the Catholic tradition. The crescent moon's symbol of Diana became associated with the Madonna, thus making the crescent shape an icon of nurturing and protection. The *corno/cornu*, is the crescent shape of a bulls horn, although the dried chili pepper shape is often found to depict a horn. The chili pepper is used because of its red color, a color believed to possess the qualities of energy, strength, power, passion, and fortune. Red is considered to be the earth color that symbolizes being tied to the earth. (See **COLORS**)

The hand can shape the horn, *mano cornuto*, sign pointing it down to keep away the evil eye. If one aims the *mano cornuto* at one's face, then he/she is saying that person's wife is being unfaithful to him. This horn shape is made with the small finger and the index finger extended while the thumb holds the middle finger and the ring finger. There are certain other hand positions, called *mudras* from ancient Eastern teachings, which can keep the *malocchio* at bay. The upright hand as in swearing an oath is said to be effective. The hand shape we see priests use for benedictions where the index, middle finger and thumb are held straight up, tightly closed, while the ring finger and little finger are folding under the hand, is also useful. The two hands held up in the position of worship and prayer comes from an ancient charm that was used against the evil eye.

There are any number of physical actions, plant uses, medals, metals, coins, minerals, salts, stones, crystals, animal parts and skins, insects, potions, chants, prayers, and others that have been used to combat the curses of the evil eye. One rarely recognized antidote to the *malocchio* is spittle. We spit on dice for luck. We spit on our hands to begin a hard task. We spit on our baseball gloves to get it ready to catch. It is said that licking a wart every morning will cause it to go away. Moms used to use their saliva to rub away sprains or cuts on their children. In ancient times the most common action against a person one suspected of being the evil eye was to spit into one's own bosoms three times. It is written that Christ healed a blind man by spitting on the ground, mixing the clay with his spittle, and then anointing the man's eyes with the mixture. Nurse maids looking after infants were to spit three times on the floor as they viewed the sleeping child. The act of spitting at one's feet or directly at them is considered to be an act of contempt these days, but the act possibly began as a way to shield oneself from a perceived evilness in an adversary standing before him/her. Mark Hehl tells of living in the Bushwick section of Brooklyn, New York, when he was a child and his parents and a neighbor had a quarrel that was unresolved so that the neighbor made a point to spit on the pavement in the front of his house whenever she passed by. Additionally, the fear of the eye is even found in the marriage ceremony. In Italy in bygone days, the groom kept a piece of metal in his pocket, usually a nail to keep away the evil eye. The bride covered her face with a veil while coming down the aisle to prevent her from inadvertently making eye contact with someone's evil eye. It is safe to say that most of the entries in this work are rooted in the beliefs, however cursory, that the evil eye forces still hover about (See *BLESSINGS*)

SERAFINO
AND THE EVIL EYE
INSPIRED BY CONTRIBUTORS

Serafino insisted nothing was wrong with him. He only had a headache he kept recanting. Grandma Cusumano had been secretly observing her grandson as he lethargically slouched on the couch the last few days, declining her cooking, responding in crisp one syllables or quiet grunts, always with petulant frowns. His parents didn't seem to be that concerned, attributing his attitude to boredom. Nonna, on the other hand was gravely concerned. She had seen this type of behavior many times before, in the old country. With all of his day-to-day activities and his freedom to come and go as he pleased with friends, especially his having sleep-overs in strangers' homes, she suspected someone had cast an evil eye on him. In talking to her *cummari* Filomena, explaining what she was witnessing, Zia Filomena concurred with her assessment and suggested she bring the boy as soon as possible. It would not be easy for Nonna to talk Serafino into going or convince his parents that she should take the boy to her old friend's house. Her daughter and son-in-law humored her old country "superstitions," but she wondered just how far they would allow her to go with taking their son to someone that, under the circumstances, they would consider a "witch." So, with much thought, Nonna came to a decision. She would not tell anyone why she was taking Serafino to her *cummari*'s house. She would ask her daughter Pina to allow Serafino to accompany her on the few blocks to Filomena's house. And so it was arranged on a Saturday that Nonna Cusumano and Serafino would walk the four blocks of the neighborhood to see Zia Filomena.

Filomena greeted the two visitors, Serafino going in before his grandmother. He was still moving slowly, begrudgingly going through the motions of greeting the old lady, and following her directions to the small dining room just past the parlor room.

"So when was the last time I saw your *niputi* Rosie? He's grown up so fast."

"*Si*. I don't remember when he came with me last to see you. He looks like his grandpa, God rest his soul, don't he?"

"*Si*. He's a good looking one, Rosie," she said as she mussed his hair a bit as though examining for lice.

Serafino didn't think much of the action, he was always being pinched, rubbed, hugged, kissed, even playfully shoved, by these old people. He knew it was part of being Italian. But then she asked him to sit in a chair with its back to the table. He dutifully followed her directions.

"Serafino. Zia Filomena is going to test to see why you're having headaches and are not eating," Nonna confessed.

Serafino looked at her quizzically.

"This won't take long and it won't hurt, but we have to find out whether someone has cast an evil eye spell on you or not."

"What's an evil eye, Nonna?"

"It's when somebody is jealous of you because you have good looks, or good at sports, or popular with everybody, or have rich parents, or a bunch of other things. They wish they could have these things, but since they don't, they cast an evil eye spell on you."

"How can they do that Nonna?" It now appeared that Serafino was beginning to get frightened over the whole matter. He looked at his grandmother and began to get glassy eyes.

"They can do it a bunch of ways; but that doesn't matter now. We got to see if you do have the eye. If so, Zia Filomena will chase it away. She knows how to do that."

Serafino sat there and waited for what might come. His grandma, held his hand and smiled in assurance that he would be all right in the end.

Zia Filomena reached into her cupboard and took out a wide shallow bowl and handed it to Nonna Cusumano. She told her to hold the bowl and rest it on Serafino's head. Then Zia Filomena carefully poured water from a pitcher into the bowl. She then got a coffee cup and poured olive oil into it. As she walked to the front of Serafino, he could see that she dipped her right hand into the cup of olive oil and stood over him. Nonna could see that Filomena slowly let the oil drip from her fingers into the water. There was complete silence. Serafino could see Zia dip her hand into the cup again. Still silence.

"You see the drops. They hit the water and stay in one place. Both times I did this they stayed in the same shape. If they would have gotten wider or disappeared then the boy would surely have the spell, but it looks like he doesn't have the spell, *grazii 'l Signore*."

"You're sure, Mena."

"I'm sure. But just to be sure, I'll say the prayer over him."

"I'd like that," said Nonna.

Zia Filomena began, " Occhi e contro occhi e perticelli agli occhi.

Crepa l'invidia e schiattono gli occhi (Eyes and against eyes and the little opening to the eyes. Envy splits and eyes burst).

"How do you feel, Serafino?" Zia asked.

Serafino was so relieved that he didn't have this affliction called the evil eye that he forgot all about his headache. Of course, the large piece of coconut cream pie and glass of milk also helped and they seemed to have revived his taste for food.

Nonna's daughter was very upset with her mother for putting her innocent son through the ordeal of testing for the evil eye. She would not tell her husband about it just yet and she asked Serafino to hold off telling his father about it. Rather, Serafino considered the whole episode as "cool" and would certainly explain the evil eye and the magic used to detect it to his friends.

And so, in the evening when Pina's husband came home, he was bent over slightly, holding on to his forehead complaining of having a splitting headache. As Pina stepped toward the pantry to get an aspirin, she stared hard at her mother making sure Nonna Cusumano got the warning.

• MENSTRUATION •

• *A woman who is menstruating should not help with canning or jarring or else the jars will spoil.*

As found in Gambino's *Blood of My Blood*, in the old country times, menstruating woman were regarded as being under a mild curse and so they were forbidden to handle food at that time. This idea by the way is still existent in the Hindu culture where women are not allowed in some temples or allowed to handle food.

• *Girls having their periods should not touch or go near plants. The plant will die if they do so.*

Plants do not discriminate. They thrive on good care, like all of us, irrespective of who it comes from.

• MIRRORS •

- *Don't let a baby look into a mirror for a year.*

It was believed that the mirror was a gift from God; however, some cultures believed it was a collector of souls. It would not be good to let an infant look into a mirror lest the mirror capture its new and vulnerable soul.

- *Cover all mirrors after a death.*

Mirrors were used by magicians and sorcerers to tell the future and to cast spells. The early mirrors were shallow water bowls where the magician/sorcerer looked onto the water's surface. It was also believed that mirrors were able to collect the souls of the living and souls of the dead, so it was thought best to cover them after a death so the gathered souls in the mirrors were unable to escape and haunt you. There was also the notion that with a death all vanity, all care for earthly beauty has ended for the deceased. The covered mirror signifies its uselessness to the departed one.

- *Cover mirrors during a storm.*

It is probable that the adage of covering mirrors during a storm also has something to do with the magical powers of a mirror to hold an image, in this case, the image of the storm, a menacing entity. Additionally, the mirror duplicates an image and by covering it, one prevents it from duplicating the image of the storm, thus doubling its intensity.

• *Cover all mirrors on Good Friday.*

Good Friday was a day the family did not play a radio, watch television, go shopping, visit others, eat meat, etc. It was a day of quiet contemplation to acknowledge the sacred gravity of Christ's death. The day culminated with the Good Friday mass. The Church usually covered all of its statues in purple shrouds during lent, purple being the penitential color. The images were covered for the purpose of allowing congregants to focus on the Passion and death of Christ, without being distracted by the usual figures all around. It is probable that the adage to cover mirrors on Good Friday is an effort to avoid individuals from vainly viewing themselves in the mirrors rather than respecting the image of Christ. Also, Good Friday does commemorate Christ's death and so the maxim of covering a mirror after a death would apply here.

THE IMP IN THE MIRROR
BASED ON THE STORY BY ANTONIO FOGAZZARO (1842-1911)

Once upon a time, there lived in Milan a very rich countess who loved to entertain her friends. Since the countess had a fabulous cook and a cellar of the finest wines, very few ever refused her invitations. One evening she invited eleven guests to her home: a young widow, an English lady, a court judge, a portly general, a handsome young lieutenant, a longhaired composer, a starving poet, and four handsome young men who fully occupied themselves with doing nothing but looking handsome. On this particular night, the topic of conversation led to the eternally argued topic of the vanity of men compared to that of women. The women declared that men were the vainer sex and by way of proving their point they claimed that men were ever incapable of passing a mirror without admiring their image. The men protested and the general luridly declared that men might be vain, but it was usually based on other features of their anatomy beyond their looks. At this statement there was a loud screech of laughter. The men assumed it was one of the women and each of the women assumed it was one or the other. Truth be told, it was none of the ladies in the room. It was an imp. Imps are good at hiding anywhere and doing mischief no matter where they are. This imp, hearing the talk, decided he would hide in the hall mirror. You see, the countess's grand quarters had two hallways that met at a right angle, and a tall mirror was fitted at the corner. No one could walk through those halls without seeing the mirror and guests were obliged to walk through those halls to use the toilets.

The night went on with fellow feelings, good food, and liberal glasses of wine; and one by one, as is natural, each guess had to use the toilet. The general was first to weave his way out of the dining room and walk along one of the halls. As he neared the restroom, he chanced to glance at the mirror in the corner. He walked closer to it to see himself better, and to his chagrin, he saw an ink stain on his left cheek. The general forgot about the restroom and, holding a handkerchief to his face, he hastened to find the butler to ask him for a bowl of water and a towel. Soon, the judge needed to use the toilet and he too succumbed to the mirror's spell and to his horror, he found there was an ink blotch on his left cheek. He darted away toward the butler's quarters and implored him to give him a towel with which to wipe his face clean. Soon, the lieutenant was asking the butler for something to wash his face, claiming he smudged his face with a soiled glove. The musician followed, claiming he inadvertently marked his face with one of his manuscript quills. Then came the poet, who surmised that he must have splashed ink from his ink well onto his face. The butler was overwhelmed by the men coming to him asking for towels to wipe their faces to the point of having run out of rooms in which to put the men who frantically wiped their left cheeks while nudging each other aside to ask whether their spot was gone.

Presently, each man returned to the dining room, all of them showing red marks on their left cheeks. The ladies asked them to give reasons for their conditions. Each man's explanation fell short of reasoning and after further hemming and hawing, each had to admit that while inspecting his image in the mirror he had discovered a mark on his face. To be sure the ladies believed this last version of his explanation, the judge asked the butler to corroborate his and the others' stories. The butler, in all humility, had to declare that he never saw a mark on any of the men's faces. Then the loud laughter came again from nowhere and everywhere. It was the imp who shouted:

> BEHIND THE MIRROR WHERE I DWELL;
>> THOSE STAINS ARE THE SORT OF LIES I TELL.
> BUT ALL THE LIES YOU'VE HEARD SINCE THEN.
>> WERE UTTERED BY THESE GENTLEMEN.

• MONEY •

- *Bury your money in your back yard.*

In my youth, Italian family gatherings always got around to specu-
lations about where "the old man" (my grandfather) buried his money. He
was a farmer and everyone believed that he must have hidden it under his
barn. Diggings under there never uncovered any such treasure. Whether
he did or did not, we will never know. The Sicilian temperament is one
of distrust of authority and institutions, so it is conceivable that "the old
man" did bury his money somewhere. My own father eventually fessed up
to having a cache hidden in his utility room's ceiling. We painstakingly
talked him into investing it; but we don't know whether he may have had
another stash buried in the backyard.

It can't be said for sure that Great-grandmother Rosa buried her
money in the backyard, but Louisa Calio's piece, *Great Grandmother Rosa a
Medial Woman*, tells us where she kept it:

"Rosa was the practical balance to her husband Luigi, a grocer
who lost his business giving people credit. He ended up a rag man, but no
matter how humble and poor insisted that they invite less fortunate people
in on every holiday for supper... [W]hen he was totally broke he took to
his bed and was ready to give up on life. Rosa came to his rescue and asked
Luigi what it would take for him to start again. Money, he said, [he] would
need money to start over and sell groceries. She reportedly went into her
large bosom and pulled out several hundred dollars, so said my mother,
which she had gathered from pennies saved over a lifetime and gave to
him to begin again."

- *Throw change in the back of a new car.*

This no doubt is a modern custom. I don't think coins were thrown into the back seat of a chariot in ancient Rome. That said, the ancients did attribute good luck to gold and while coins are no longer made of gold, the idea of good luck continues to be associated with coins. Also, coins are metal and metal has always been a talisman to ward off bad luck.

- *Always put some money into a wallet or purse when given as presents.*

In the days of the hand-operated water pump, one needed to prime the pump with a bucket of water to get the water to flow. This is the same principle of priming to get money to flow.

Putting money into a new money holder is the primer for eventual money in-flow. It is a means of affirming that more riches are to follow.

- *When your palms itch that means money is coming.*

As mentioned in my introduction, this adage depends on which hand has the itch.

If the right-hand itches, money is coming. If the left-hand itches, money is going to be spent or lost.

(See **RIGHT VS LEFT** and **INTRODUCTION**)

- *Do not allow your purse or pocketbook to rest on the floor or you will always be without money.*

There is also a Chinese proverb that says, "A purse on the floor is money out the door."

The basis of this saying may have something to do with the cavalier treatment of an object that is used to store money. Money symbolizes one's work and prosperity. If one is so careless as to leave this money container out of reach, or on the floor, a place of baseness, then the disrespect is sure to cause other carelessness, which may lead to a loss of what they have.

- *Money on the kitchen table brings bad luck.*

The kitchen table is meant for family gatherings and eating meals. It is said that shaking hands across the kitchen table brings on bad luck because business is being transacted where it shouldn't be. This would seem to apply to money sitting on the table. Money is unclean, being handled by so many people, and it is out of place and sullies the dedicated family space. In ancient Roman beliefs, three angels always guarded the house. One looked over the door, one looked over the bed, and the other kept watch over the table. These places were considered sacrosanct parts of a home that might bring on bad luck if misused.

- *Sweep money out of your door then back into your door three times to insure you always have money.*

Here the "three times" implies, "The third time is the charm." As mentioned before, often the threshold is ignored in these types of "doorway" idioms. It could be that passing one's money over the threshold (See **DOORS AND CHARMS**) is a way of magnetizing it so that it draws more money to itself.

- *Unexpected money may come to you under a full moon.*

The moon is thought to have many mystical powers, chief among them is its gravitation pull. We are all aware how the moon creates the tides from this force, so there is also the idea that the moon could possibly draw money into our life. Then too, it is a fact that one might be able to see dropped money by the light of the full moon whereas he/she might have missed it on other nights.

- *Tape a quarter over a new-born baby's belly button to keep it from protruding.* (See **BABIES**)

- *Don't spend money on New Year's Day or you will be spending for the rest of the year.* (See **NEW YEAR**)

- *If one spends too much money on New Year's Day, he/she is seemingly resolving to spend money for the rest of the year.* (See **NEW YEAR**)

- *A fool and his money are soon parted.*

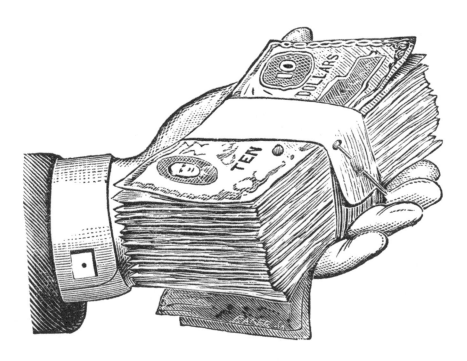

HARD TIMES.
A TARANTELLA TALE
AS TOLD BY VINCENTIA CACIBAUDA (1917-2002)

Lamp aglow in
casa evenings
Nonna Pina's
Story to spin.
Children gathered
All around her
Faces beaming
Then she'd begin.

'Momma Momma'
They did cry out
'Why you hide your
Money that way?'
'It's for hard times
That may soon come
So I have to
Save for the day.'

"Once a woman
Not an old one
Had two Children
Not very bright.
She wove baskets
Sold them quickly
Hid the money
Out of plain sight.

Nonna mentioned
She did stress
Guisepp' and Rosa
Had pasta for brains
Blabbed to their friends
Of the money
Saved for hard times
Hidden away.

Giuseppuzzu
Rosalina
Spied her open
A coffee can.
Stuff her money
Most her earnings
What was left she
Paid the tax man

Now it happened
That a classmate
Guido Latru
Heard of the can.
Told his uncle
There was money
He might eas'ly
Get in his hands

Ziu Latru
Hid in shadows
Watching Momma
Leave for the day.
When she did leave
Ziu Latru
Crept up slowly
Sizing his prey

'Oh my children
My sweet children
Is your momma
Available, my dears?'
'She has left sir,'
Said the two kids
'Well she asked I
Meet her right here.

I'm expected
Did she tell you?
I do need the
Money you see.
I am Hard Times
Now please tell me
Where the hidden
money mighty be.

Rosalina
and Giuseppe
So well mannered
Obedient too.
Got the can that
Mom had hidden
Brought it to him
'It's all for you.'

'Momma Momma'
They were so proud
We have something
Special to say.
While you were gone
Mister Hard Times
Came to take his
Money away.'

"Did she beat those
Naughty children?"
Nonna Pina's
Niputi asked.
"What would you do?"
Said their Nonna.
Think about it
It's time for bed."

· MOON ·

There is a Calabrian story that goes like this:

    The moon used to be a woman bread maker whose face gleaned with the reflection of the oven. One day she annoyed her mother, and her mother took the brushes used to clean the ashes from the oven and smudged her face.

                    — Douglas

- *Sleeping under a full moon will cause you to become crazy.*

The words "lunatic, loony," come from the word *luna*, the latin word for "*Moon*":

    It is often thought that because the moon acts on large bodies of water to create tides, and our bodies are 60 to 80 percent water, that the moon affects our bodies; but the Farmer's Almanac tells us this is not the case. Perhaps one sleeping under the brightness of the moon might become ditzy in the morning from a lack of sleep, but the condition should go away with a night's proper sleep in the dark. Women's menstrual cycles last about 28 days which closely coincide with the 29 days of the lunar phase; but studies show this is only coincidental and not causative. Also, there are anecdotal claims that there are more crimes, riots, emergency calls, etc. on full moon nights than other nights; but actual research says that this is not so (*Almanac.com*).

- *Cut your hair when the moon is full and it will grow faster.* (See **HAIR**)

- *Unexpected money may come to you under a full moon.* (See **MONEY**)

DIALOGUE BETWEEN THE EARTH AND THE MOON
FROM "DIALOGUES" BY GIACOMO LEOPARDI (1798-1837)

Earth: Dear Moon, I know that you can speak and answer questions like a human being, for I have heard so from many of the poets. Besides, our children say you have really a mouth, nose, and eyes like everyone else, and that they see them with their own eyes, which at their time of life ought to be very sharp. As for me, no doubt you know that I am a person; indeed, when I was young, I had a number of children; so, you will not be surprised to hear me speak. And the reason, my fine Moon, why I have never uttered a word to you before, although I have been your neighbor for I don't know how many centuries, is that I have been so occupied as to have no time for gossip. But now my business is so trifling that it can look after itself. I don't know what to do, and am ready to die of boredom. So, in the future, I hope we may often have some talk together; and I should like to know all about your affairs, if it does not inconvenience you to recount them to me.

Moon: Be easy on that score. May the Fates never trouble me more than you are likely to! Talk as much as you please, and although, as I believe you know, I am partial to silence, I will willingly listen and reply, to oblige you.

Earth: Do you hear the delightful sound made by the heavenly bodies in motion?

Moon: To tell you the truth, I hear nothing.

Earth: Nor do I; save only the whistling of the wind, which blows from my poles to the equator, and from the equator to the poles, and which is far from musical. But Pythagoras asserts that the celestial spheres make an incredibly sweet harmony, and that you take part in the concert, and are the eighth chord of this universal lyre. As for me, I am so deafened by my own noise that I hear nothing.

Moon: I also am doubtless deafened, since I hear no more than you. But it is news to me that I am a chord.

Earth: Now let us change the subject. Tell me; are you really inhabited, as thousands of ancient and modern philosophers affirm—from Orpheus to De Lalande* In spite of all my efforts to prolong these horns of mine, which men call mountains and hills, and from the summits of which I look at you in silence, I have failed to discern a single one of your inhabitants. Yet I am told that a certain David Fabricius**, whose eyes were keener than those of Lynceus***, at one time observed your people extending their linen to be dried by the sun.

Moon: I know nothing about your horns. I will admit that I am inhabited.

Earth: What color are your men?

Moon: What men?

Earth: Those that you contain. Did you not say you were inhabited?

Moon: Yes, what then?

Earth: Does it not follow that all your inhabitants are animals?

Moon: Neither animals nor men, though I am really in ignorance as to the nature of either the one or the other. As for the men you speak of, I have not an idea what you mean.

Earth: Then what sorts of creatures are yours?

Moon: They are of very many different kinds, as unknown to you, as yours are to me.

Earth: This is so strange that if you yourself had not informed me of it, I would never have believed it. Were you ever conquered by any of your inhabitants?

Moon: Not that I know of. But how? And for what reason?

Earth: Through ambition and jealousy; by means of diplomacy and arms.

Moon: I do not know what you mean by arms, ambition, and diplomacy. Indeed, I understand nothing of what you say.

Earth: But surely if you do not understand the meaning of arms, you know something of war; because, not long ago, a certain doctor discovered through a telescope, which is an instrument for seeing a long distance, that you possessed a fine fortress with proper bastions. Now this is certain proof that your races are at any rate accustomed to sieges and mural battles.

Moon: Pardon me, Mother Earth, if I reply to you a little more at length than would be expected from one so subjugated as it seems I am. But in truth, you appear to me more than vain to imagine that everything in the world is conformable to your things; as if Nature had no other intention than to copy you exactly in each of her creations. I tell you I am inhabited, and you jump to the conclusion that my inhabitants are men. I assert that they are not, and while admitting that they may be another race of beings, you endow them with qualities and customs similar to those of your people. You also speak to me about the telescope of a certain doctor. But it seems to me the sight of these telescopes is about as good as that of your children, who discover that I have eyes, a mouth, and a nose, all of which I am ignorant of possessing.

Earth: Then it is not true that your provinces are intersected by fine long roads, and that you are cultivated? Those things are clearly discernible with a telescope from Germany.

Moon: I do not know whether I am cultivated, and I have never observed my roads.

Earth: Dear Moon, you must know that I am of a coarse composition, and very simple-minded. No wonder therefore that men easily deceive me. But I can assure you that if your own inhabitants do not care to conquer you, you are by no means free from such danger; for at different times many people down here have thought of subduing you, and have even made great preparations for doing so. Some have tried to reach you by going to my highest places, standing on tiptoe, and stretching out their arms. Besides, they have made a careful study of your surface, and drawn-out maps of your countries. They also know the heights of your mountains, and even their names. I warn you of these things out of pure goodwill, so that you may be prepared for any emergency. Now, permit me to ask you another question or two. Are you much disturbed by the dogs that bay at you? What do you think of those people who show you another moon in a well? Are you masculine or feminine? Because anciently there was a difference of opinion about that. Is it true that the Arcadians came into the world before you? Are your women, or whatever I should call them, oviparous, and did one of their eggs fall down to us, once upon a time? Are you perforated like a bead, as a modern philosopher believes? Are you made of green cheese, as some English say? Is it true that Mahomet one fine night cut you in two like a water melon, and that a good piece of your body fell into his cloak? Why do you like to stay on the tops of minarets? What do you think of the feast of Bairam?

Moon: You may as well go on. I need not answer such questions, nor depart from my accustomed habit of silence. If you wish to be so frivolous, and can find nothing else to talk to me about except matters incomprehensible to me, your people had better construct another planet to rotate round them, which they can design and populate as they please. You seem unable to talk of anything but men, and dogs, and such things, of which I know as much as of that one great being round which I am told our sun turns.

Earth: Truly, the more I determine not to touch on personal matters, the less I succeed in my resolution. But for the future I will be more careful. Tell me; do you amuse yourself by drawing up my sea-water, and then letting it fall again?

Moon: It may be. But if I have done this, or other such things, I am unaware of it. And you, it seems to me, do not consider what you effect here, which is of so much the more importance as your size and strength are greater than mine.

Earth: I know nothing of these effects, except that from time to time I deprive you of the sun's light, and myself of yours, and that I illumine you during your nights, as is sometimes evident to me. But I am forgetting one thing, which is the most important of all. I should like to know if Ariosto is correct in saying that everything man loses, such as youth, beauty, health, the vigor and money spent in the pursuit of glory, in the instruction of children, and founding or promoting useful institutions, flies to you; so that you possess all things pertaining to man, except folly, which has never left mankind. If this be true, I reckon you ought to be so full as to have scarcely any space unoccupied, especially since men have recently lost a great many things (such as patriotism, virtue, magnanimity, righteousness), not merely in part, or singly, as in former times, but completely, and without exception. And certainly, if you have not got these things, I do not know where else they can be. But supposing you have them, I wish we could come to an agreement whereby you might soon return the lost things to me; for I imagine you must be greatly encumbered, especially with common sense, which I understand crowds you very much. In return for this, I will see that men pay you annually a good sum of money.

Moon: Men again! Though folly, as you say, has not left your domains, you wish nevertheless to make an utter fool of me, by depriving me of what reason I possess, to supply the deficiency in your people. But I do not know where this reason of yours is, or whether it can be found in the universe. I know well that it is not here, any more than the other things you mention.

Earth: At least, you can tell me if your inhabitants are acquainted with vices, misdeeds, misfortunes, suffering, and old age; in short, evils? Do you understand these names?

Moon: Yes, I understand these well enough, and not only the names. I am full of them, instead of the other things.

Earth: Which are the more numerous among your people, virtues or vices?

Moon: Vices, by a long way.

Earth: Does pleasure or pain predominate?

Moon: Pain is infinitely more prevalent.

Earth: And your inhabitants, are they mostly happy or unhappy?

Moon: So unhappy that I would not exchange my lot with the happiest of them.

Earth: It is the same here. I wonder why we differ so much in other things, yet agree in this.

Moon: I am also like you in shape, I rotate like you, and am illumined by the same sun. It is no more wonderful that we should resemble each other in these things, than that we should possess common failings; because evil is as common to all the planets of the universe, or at least of the solar system, as rotundity, movement, and light. And if you could speak loud enough for Uranus or Saturn, or any other planet, to hear you, and were to ask them if they contained unhappiness, and whether pleasure or pain predominated, each would answer as I have done. I speak from experience, for I have already questioned Venus and Mercury, to whom I am now and then nearer than you. I have also asked certain comets that have passed by me; they all replied to the same effect. I firmly believe even the sun and every star would make the same response.

Earth: Still I am very hopeful. In future I trust men will permit me to experience much happiness.

Moon: Hope as much as you please. I will answer for it you may hope for ever.

Earth: Ha! Did you hear that? These men and animals of mine are making an uproar. It is night on the side from which I am speaking to you, and at first they were all asleep. But, thanks to our conversation, they are now wide awake, and very frightened.

Moon: And here, on the other side, you see it is day.

Earth: Yes. Now I do not wish to terrify my people, or interrupt their sleep, which is the best thing they possess; so let us postpone conversation until another opportunity. Adieu, and good-day to you.

Moon: Adieu. Good-night.

---

* Composer; 1657.

** Astronomist; c1596.

*** Lynceus was the look-out on the Argo, the ship on which Jason and the Argonauts sailed to retrieve the Golden Fleece.

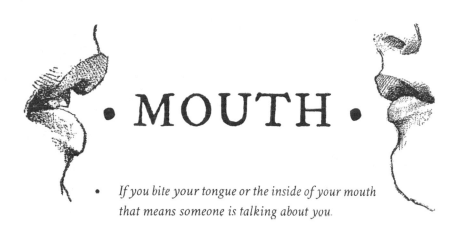

MOUTH

- *If you bite your tongue or the inside of your mouth that means someone is talking about you.*

This idea is similar to the idea that if your ear itches or you hear a whistle, someone is saying something about you.

- *If your nose itches, someone wants to kiss you.*

It is based on the idea that we are always subconsciously aware of what is going on around us and our bodies react subconsciously. The acuteness of early man's senses was a factor in his survival, and no doubt his awareness of the things around him were as keen as animals are today. Animals have kept their keen senses; we humans deny most of our intuitions. The concept of the evil eye is based on the notion that there are some who have the ability to affect others at a distance. So, in this sense, one who accidentally bites his/her tongue, or the inside of his/her mouth does have the option of blaming the event on someone else.

- *If a bee or spider should get on you, put your tongue to the left side of your mouth and they won't bite you.*

It is possible here that placing one's tongue in that part of the mouth doesn't allow a person to yell or scream thus keeping them from exciting the insects to point of attacking. It is known that blowing at a bee or flying insect disturbs its sense of direction and causes it to go away. Blowing hard on a spider might cause it to drop off. However, blowing is not possible with the tongue rooted to the left side of the mouth. There may be some merit in not just touching the tongue to the side of the cheek, but pushing the tongue so that the cheek bulges out. The mere sight of a human face distorted by this pose might, like Miss Muffet, frighten the spider away.

- *Dreaming of back teeth falling out means you will learn of a death.* (See **DEATH**)

· NEW YEAR ·

- *It was the custom in Sicily to wear red underwear from New Year's Eve to New Year's Day.* (See **COLORS**)

- *Don't serve chicken on New Year's Day.*

Chickens scratch from front to back symbolizing moving good luck away (Sweeping out good luck with a broom). Also, chickens are scavengers implying that they never have what they need and must continually scratch and search to survive. Perhaps the chicken's negative portrayal (admittedly on display as it rests in the middle of the table) far outweighs its tastiness on that particular day.

- *Don't spend money on New Year's Day or you will be spending for the rest of the year.*

- *If one spends too much money on New Year's Day, he/she is seemingly resolving to spend money for the rest of the year.*

A new year has always held a special feeling of change about it. In this respect, whatever you do on the first day is thought to set the trend for the coming year. This is the reasoning behind a New Year resolution. It is designed to be a template of your conduct in the coming year.

- *Don't wash clothes on New Year's Day or you will be washing clothes to go to a funeral.*

The idea here is that washing clothes on the first day of the year may symbolize washing away a family member. It is probable that this proverb goes as far as predicting which member is lost according to whose clothing is washed first or last; or whose piece of clothing dries first, or happens to fall off the clothes line.

- *Don't sweep the floor on New Year's Day or someone might leave the house forever.*

There is the warning that sweeping the floor means that you are sweeping out good luck along with the dust of the home. It appears that this is the same reasoning as the idea of washing clothes on New Year's Day. That is, sweeping the floor could lead to metaphorically sweeping family member out of the door.

- *My father would go out in the back yard and shoot his shot gun into the air for the New Year.*

The fired rifle performs the same function as the start of the New Year noise makers. The idea is to make a racket designed to chase away the evil spirits who are also celebrating the New Year. The Chinese are thought to be the first to celebrate the New Year and they used fireworks for their noise makers either to get the attention of the gods, or to chase away evil spirits

NEW YEAR

LAURA RICHARDS (1850-1943)

The little sweet Child tied on her hood, and put on her warm cloak and mittens.

"I am going to the wood," she said, "to tell the creatures all about it. They cannot understand about Christmas, mamma says, and of course she knows, but I do think they ought to know about New Year!"

Out in the wood the snow lay light and powdery on the branches, but underfoot it made a firm, smooth floor, over which the Child could walk lightly without sinking in. She saw other footprints beside her own, tiny bird-tracks, little hopping marks, which showed where a rabbit had taken his way, traces of mice and squirrels and other little wild-wood beasts.

The child stood under a great hemlock-tree, and looked up toward the clear blue sky, which shone far away beyond the dark tree-tops. She spread her hands abroad and called, "Happy New Year! Happy New Year to everybody in the wood, and all over the world!"

A rustling was heard in the hemlock branches, and a striped squirrel peeped down at her. "What do you mean by that, little Child?" he asked. And then from all around came other squirrels, came little field-mice, and hares swiftly leaping, and all the winter birds, titmouse and snow-bird, and many another; and they all wanted to know what the Child meant by her greeting, for they had never heard the words before.

"It means that God is giving us another year!" said the Child. "Four more seasons, each lovelier than the last, just as it was last year. Flowers will bud, and then they will blossom, and then the fruit will hang all red and golden on the branches, for birds and men and little children to eat."

"And squirrels, too!" cried the chipmunk, eagerly.

"Of course!" said the Child. "Squirrels, too, and every creature that lives in the good green wood. And this is not all! We can do over again the things that we tried to do last year, and perhaps failed in doing. We have another chance to be good and kind, to do little loving things that help, and to cure ourselves of doing naughty things. Our hearts can have lovely new seasons, like the flowers and trees and all the sweet things that grow and bear leaves and fruit. I thought I would come and tell you all this, because sometimes one does not think of things till one hears them from another's lips. Are you glad I came? If you are glad, say Happy New Year! each in his own way! I say it to you all now in my way. Happy New Year! Happy New Year!"

Such a noise as broke out then had never been heard in the wood since the oldest hemlock was a baby, and that was a long time ago. Chirping, twittering, squeaking, chattering! The wood-doves lit on the Child's shoulder and cooed in her ear, and she knew just what they said. The squirrels made a long speech, and meant every word of it, which is more than people always do; the field-mouse said that she was going to turn over a new leaf, the very biggest cabbage-leaf she could find; while the titmouse invited the whole company to dine with him, a thing he had never done in his life before.

When the Child turned to leave the wood, the joyful chorus followed her, and she went, smiling, home and told her mother all about it. "And, mother," she said, "I should not be surprised if they had got a little bit of Christmas, after all, along with their New Year!"

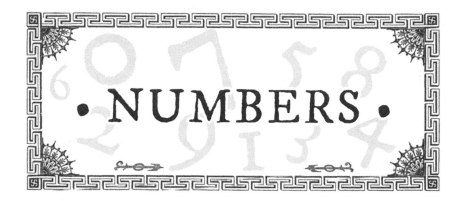

• NUMBERS •

- *If you are walking with a group and come to an obstacle in your path, you must divide the group evenly, or not at all, before going around to avoid getting bad luck.*

- *Thirteen is a lucky number (for Italians).*

- *Seventeen is an unlucky number (for Italians).*

- *Always give an odd number of roses (flowers).*

According to dpetals.wordpress.com: "In majority of countries around the world, odd numbers are considered harbingers of happiness and luck. Even Numbers are never chosen when it comes to important matters in life. Flowers are hence gifted in an odd number in order to portray the true happiness during a special occasion. An even number of flowers is used only during sad occasions like funerals." Pythagoras considered "one" the father of numbers and "two" the mother. He attributed the power of the father to odd numbers, i.e., assertive strength, and the feminine nature, i.e., unassertive, perhaps then perceived as meek qualities.

NUMBERS THREE AND SEVEN:
BALANCED AND SACRED

The numbers 7 and 3 are found in most situations in our world. Seven can be considered a sacred number, perhaps a metaphysical number to wit: Seven days of the week; Seventh day is a holy day that belongs to worship; Muslim pilgrims circle the Kaaba at Mecca seven times; creation took seven days; the number seven is mentioned in the bible more often than any, e.g. seven trumpeters circled Jericho seven times; turn your cheek 7 times 70, suggests Christ; seven locks of Samson's hair were cut. Sinbad sailed the seven seas; there are seven wonders of the world, and seven energy centers in the human body, chakras. These are but a few examples of where the number seven shows up. (numerologist.com)

The number three is often used in telling jokes where there are three particulars; three events, three people, three questions, three actions, etc., etc., etc. with the punchline landing on the third particular. The number three allows man to mark his place in space and time. Here, there, everywhere in space and, past, present, future in time. Or beginning, middle, end; birth, life, death. In space we have width, length, height; The day's stages are morning, noon, night; Christians recognize Father, Son, Holy Ghost; Hindus recognize Brahma, Vishnu, Shiva; Then there are proverbs: "Third time is a charm;" "Ready, Set, Go;" "Hip, Hip, Hooray;" "He's a jolly good fellow" times three; etc., etc., etc. (See *HOUSE MAKING*)

The number three is a balanced number. Imagine a see-saw, a lever arm, with a load at one end and the effort at the other end, with the fulcrum in the middle. The number two is an equal number, but it is not a balanced number. There must be a middle component to make two things balanced. This is why odd numbers are used most often in these sayings and in writings. In terms of geometry (space) the triangle was considered by the Egyptians as being a complete perfect figure. The superstition of avoiding walking under a ladder came from the belief that one interferes with the perfect symmetry of the triangle of ladder, wall, and ground. It is no accident that pyramids are three-dimension triangles believed to possess special energetic properties. Prayers, affirmations, chants, incantations, magic spells, all are performed three times.

LOVE OF THE THREE ORANGES
A RETELLING OF THE STORY OF THREES
ANTONIO IVE (1851-1937)

Once upon a time, there was a king and queen who had a somber son. The queen was deeply grieved at this, and she prayed to the Lord to ask counsel of him what she was to do with this son. The Lord told her to try to do something to make him laugh. Gather people around is what he suggested.

She replied: "What shall I do to get them to gather!"

The Lord said to her: "Give away something."

"But I have nothing to give but oil," said the queen.

"Then give this oil away to those who come, for there will be people with many different looks, some with big noses, others with skinny necks, some fat jowls, other bodies as skinny as a nail, and it may happen that your son will see someone that will make him laugh."

So, the queen proclaimed that she had a vat of oil, and that all could come and take some. And everybody, indeed, hurried there and took the oil down to the last drop. Last of all came an old witch, who begged the queen to give her a little, saying: "Give me a little oil, too!"

The queen replied: "Ah, it is all gone, there is no more!" The queen was not happy that her son had not yet laughed and was still somber.

The old witch said again to the queen: "Let me look in the vat!"

The queen opened the vat, and the old woman got inside of it and was all covered with the dregs of the oil. Seeing this, the prince laughed, and laughed, and laughed. The old woman came out, saw the prince laughing, and said to him: "True you laugh, but you will not be happy until you go and find the Love of the three Oranges."

The son, his curiosity piqued, said to his mother: "Ah, mother, I shall have no more peace until I go and find the Love of the three Oranges."

She answered: "My dear son, how will you go and find the Love of the three Oranges?" He could not say, but he would go. So, he mounted his horse and rode, and rode, and rode until he came to a large gate.

He knocked, and someone within asked: "Who is there?"

He re plied: "A soul created by God."

The one within said: "In all the years that I have been here no one has ever knocked at this gate."

The prince repeated: "Open, for I am a soul created by God!"

Then an old man came down and opened the gate. The old man asked: "Where are you going, my son?"

"I am going to find the Love of the three Oranges."

The old man said: "The way is very dangerous, take these three twigs; you will meet some witches who are sweeping out their oven with their hands; give them these twigs, and they will let you pass."

The prince very gratefully took the twigs, mounted his horse, and rode away. He journeyed a long time, and at last saw in the distance three witches of immense size coming towards him. He threw them the twigs, and they allowed him to pass. He continued his journey, and arrived at a gate larger than the first. Here the same thing occurred as at the first one, and the old man said:

"The way is very dangerous, take these three ropes, for you will encounter some witches drawing water with their tresses; throw them these ropes, and they will let you pass."

Everything happened as the old man said; the prince passed the witches and continued his journey. He came to a third gate that was larger than the second. Here an old man gave him a bag of bread, and one of tallow, saying:

"Take this bag of bread; you will meet three large dogs: throw them the bread and they will let you pass; then you will come to a large gate with many rusty padlocks; then you will see a tower, and in it you will find the Love of the three Oranges. When you reach that place, take this tallow and oil well the rusty padlocks; and when you have ascended the tower, you will find the oranges hanging from a nail. There will also be an old woman. She has a son who is an ogre and eats Christians. You must be very careful!"

The prince, well contented, took the bag of bread and the tallow and rode away. After a long journey, he saw at a distance three great dogs with their mouths wide open coming to eat him. He threw them the bread, and they let him pass. He journeyed on until he came to another large gate with many rusty padlocks. He dismounted, tied his horse to the gate, and began to anoint the locks with the tallow, until, after much creaking, they opened. The prince entered, saw the tower, went up and met an old woman who said to him:

"Dear son, why are you here? My son the ogre will surely eat you up." Hearing her son come running toward her, the old woman made the prince hide under the bed; but the ogre perceived that there was someone in the house. He sniffed and sniffed and began to chant:

"I smell a Christian; I smell a Christian!"

"Oh, my son," his mother said, "there is no one here."

But he repeated his cry. "I smell a Christian; I smell a Christian."

Then his mother, to quiet him, threw him a piece of meat, which he ate like a madman; and while he was busy eating, she gave the three oranges to the prince, saying:

"Take them and escape at once, for he will soon finish eating his meat, and then he will want to eat you."

After she had given him the three oranges, she thought about how angry her son would be for her allowing the Christian to go free; and so, she had a change of heart, crying out: "Stairs, throw him down! Locks close him in!"

The locks answered: "We will not, for he gave us tallow!"

Then she yelled: "Dogs, devour him!"

The dogs said: "We will not, for he gave us bread!"

Quickly the prince mounted his horse and rode away as the old woman continued to cry after him: "Witch, strangle him!""

"I will not, for he gave me ropes to draw our water!"

"Witches, burn him!"

"We will not, for he gave us twigs to clean our ovens!"

The prince continued his journey with the three oranges. He soon became thirsty. He thought of the oranges and opened one to drink its juice. Once the orange was opened a beautiful girl came out saying, "Love, give me something to drink."

He replied, "Love, I have nothing to give."

And she said: "Love, I shall die!" And she died at once.

The prince threw away the orange, and continued his journey, and soon became thirsty again. In despair he opened another orange, and out sprang another girl more beautiful than the first. She, too, asked for water, and died when the prince told her he had none to give. Then he continued his way, saying:

"The next time I surely do not want to lose her.'"

When he became thirsty again, he waited until he reached a well; then he opened the last orange and there appeared a girl more beautiful than the first two. When she asked for water, he gave her the water of the well; then took her out of the orange, put her on horseback with himself, and started for home.

The young girl tired of the ride and asked if they could rest. The prince agreed and rode into a grove of beautiful trees of gold and silver leaves that produced gold and silver fruit. He made a soft couch for her and left her to rest while he rode to tell his mother of the great news of finding his love.

Presently an old hag happened on the beautiful girl resting among the trees and greeted her:

"Ah, my dear. You have such beautiful hair. Allow me to comb it."

"I do not wish it," said the girl.

"But I will make you look even more beautiful for your handsome prince."

"I do not wish it," repeated the girl.

Finally, after constant prodding with reasons why she should let the old hag comb her hair, the young girl allowed her to comb it. And what did the old crone do but put three magic hairpins in the girl's hair that turned her into a dove. Releasing the dove to the air, the old hag placed herself onto the couch of gold and silver leaves.

Meanwhile, the prince reaching home told his mother where he had left his new bride-to-be. His mother was so excited that she quickly invited many guests to celebrate the engagement and she sent a coach with seven coachmen out to get her and bring her back to celebrate. The coachmen soon arrived with the old hag. Seeing the old woman, the queen dared not say anything negative about her, fearing she would upset her son. At last, seeing the old lady, the prince assumed that through the special magic of the oranges, she had become old. With all the invited guest waiting and expecting a wedding, his family could do nothing but go through with the ceremony.

"If she came from one of the three oranges as a beautiful girl, she will once again become a beautiful woman," his mother assured him. But the prince was not convinced and began to pine away so much so that he could not bear to consider eating or drinking anything at the banquet.

As everyone seated themselves around the long dining room tables in readiness for the main meal, the beautiful girl, now a dove, flew into the cook's kitchen and sang a song that put him to sleep.

> LET THE COOK FALL ASLEEP,
> LET THE ROAST BE BURNED,
> LET THE OLD WITCH BE UNABLE TO EAT.

Everyone waited for the food, but it never came. The maids went into the kitchen and found the cook fast asleep. He had not even begun to cook. The prince, losing patience, stormed into the kitchen and demanded to know why the cook was so sleepy. The cook told him a white dove flew into his kitchen and sang such a beautiful melody that it put him to sleep. Even while the prince was there scolding him, the cook pointed to the dove as it flew past his window. The prince gave chase and seeing the bird alight on the edge of the balcony called to it. As the dove came near, the prince caught it and held it gently between his hands. It was then he saw the hairpins protruding from under its wind and carefully pulled them out one by one. With the release of the last pin, the dove transformed back into the beautiful girl he had left under the trees of gold and silver.

"Mother, mother. Honored guests. This is the beautiful girl from love of three oranges. She will be my bride."

The old hag screamed and tried to escape, but she was surrounded by the angry guests, especially after the young girl explained how she was turned into a dove by her evil magic. The guests did not treat the old woman too kindly and after having disposed of her, the prince and the maiden from the three oranges were soon joyfully married.

• OLIVE OIL •

• *Spilling olive oil is a bad omen.*

Olive oil is as sacrosanct as bread to Italians. This saying comes from the era when olive oil was a very precious and expensive commodity. Spilling any of this special possession was seen as wasting money and disrespecting the oil. Olive oil also cured ailments and was blessed for uses in special services of the Church. It is often mentioned in the Bible as an anointing agent. Since there was always the notion that evil spirits were hovering about, an accidental spill of oil would tend to expose the spiller to an attack from an evil force. Perhaps the notion by some old Sicilians that children should put a little oil in their hair to keep it from falling out might have also had the dual purpose of keeping away the evil eye and prolonging hair growth.

• *Rub injuries with olive oil.* (See **HEALING**)

• PEARLS •

- *Pearls bring on bad luck.*

This depends on how one gets the pearls. Since pearls are associated with tears, one should not gift them to another, and especially not to an engaged or newly married person with the fear that the gift will attract tears in the marriage. This association with bad luck comes from a story of an emperor who set aside a string of pearls to adorn the statue of Fortune, the Roman goddess of chance; but he changed his mind and gave the pearls to Venus, the Roman goddess of love instead, incurring the wrath of a jealous Fortune who made sure the emperor always had bad luck. On the other hand, if one buys the pearls for oneself, owing to the value of the jewels, and of course the absence of ill feelings in the transaction, then the pearls can bring on prosperity, health, luck, and good fortune. There is but one more possibility for this belief: In terms of gems, pearls exude purity and innocence to the wearer (Bergen). Since the evil eye is always attracted by purity and innocence, a bride wearing the pearls is at risk of inviting the evil eye.

• PREGNANCY •

- *Don't eat liver if you are pregnant or your child will be born with liver spots.*

- *A pregnant woman should not view or spend time around animals or the baby might look like one of them.*

- *A pregnant woman should not see ugly or scary things or the baby will look ugly or scary.*

- *A pregnant woman who craves something that is not available risks having her baby be born with a birthmark in that shape, or that color; so, she could scratch herself in a hidden place so the birthmark will not be visible on the fully clothed child.*
- *A pregnant woman should not reach her arms over her head or the cord might wrap around the baby's head.*

The word pregnant was seldom used in Sicilian homes, instead expecting women were referred to as "being in a family way" or, "in that way." Some families used the word *incinta* meaning "wearing a girdle."

Many of these warnings are ancient. Aristotle (384-322bce) wrote the following about the powers of a mother's imagination on the unborn:

"...nothing is more powerful than the imagination of the mother, for if she fix her eyes upon any object it will so impress her mind, that it oftentimes so happens that the child has a presentation there on some part of the body... The same effect has imagination in occasioning warts, stains, mole-spots... though indeed they sometimes happen through frights, or extravagant longing. Many women, in being with child, on seeing a hare cross the road in front of them will through the force of imagination, bring forth a child with a hairy lip... Therefore it behooves all women with child, if possible, to avoid, such sights, or at least, not to regard them."

These cautions, no doubt coming from older female relatives, were sincere efforts to protect the family, present and future. There were always stories of women who did not heed the warnings and paid the price. Whether Aristotle's hairy lip story was true or not is not important as the sense of fear it intended to instill in a pregnant woman lest she take her expectancy too lightly. As with all of these warnings and proverbs, the tendency is always to humor the fates, consider the axioms, and be careful.

· RIGHT ·
· VERSUS ·
· LEFT ·

(See **INTRODUCTION**)

• *One must always enter a*
  doorway with the right foot first.
  (See **DOORS**)

In ancient Rome, in homes
and in temples, the right foot was
the first foot
to enter the build-
ings. The noblemen
hired a "footman" to
stand by the door to
make sure a visitor
entered and exited
with his right foot.

The right foot was considered
the first step to begin a journey.
In fact, Pythagoras went even further
and claimed that one should always put
the right shoe on first.

Left-handed people were thought to
have a spell cast on them because there were so
few of them. Their rarities incited some people to

believe they might be wicked, or insane. The word sinister comes from the Latin word, *sinistram* which is the word for left. The French word, *gauche*, meaning unsophisticated, crude, also means left. There is an interesting book titled *The Sinister Side: How Left-Right Symbolism Shaped Western Art* by James Hall, Oxford Press, New York, 2008. Hall discusses the left-right symbolism in western culture. He addresses the left-right conventions found in classical art and in the Bible and the biases that shaped the beliefs that the right side is the positive and stronger side. Even in the rare instances where the left side is said to have positive traits, according to Plutarch (46-120AD), it is only because "the gods sent them from their right side."

- *Right palm itch, money coming.*

The right hand is considered the receiving hand and so it is a symbol of good fortune.

Isaiah 41:13 "For I, the Lord your God, hold your right hand; ... Open your right hand in order to receive God's blessing."

- *The left palm itches, money going.*

Ecclesiastes 10:2 "A wise man's heart directs him toward the right, but the foolish man's head directs him toward the left."

• SAINTS •

(See **BREAD**)

St. Joseph

St. Joseph's Day is also Father's Day all over Italy. It is celebrated on March 19th. The feast of St. Joseph is more prominent in Southern Italy, especially in Sicily, where he is its patron saint. One of the miracles ascribed to the saint was his intervention during a drought whereupon after fervent prayers, he brought on the rains sparing the crops and preventing a famine in Sicily. Is there any surprise then that he is the island's favorite saint? The following story shows just how popular he is:

THE DEVOTEE OF ST. JOSEPH
Italo Calvino (1923-1985)

Once there was a man devoted exclusively to St. Joseph. He addressed all his prayers to St. Joseph, lit candles to St. Joseph, gave alms in the name of St. Joseph; in short, he recognized no one but St. Joseph. His dying day came, and he went before St. Peter. St. Peter refused to let him in since the only things to his credit were all those prayers he had said during his lifetime to St. Joseph. He had performed no good works to speak of, and behaved as if the Lord, our Lady, and all the other saints simply did not exist.

"Since I've come all the way here," said the devotee of St. Joseph, "let me at least see him."

So St. Peter sent for St. Joseph. St. Joseph came and, finding his devotee there, said, "Bravo! I'm really pleased to have you with us. Come on in right now."

"I can't. He won't let me."

"Why not?"

"Because he says I prayed only to you and to none of the other saints."

"Well, I'll be. What difference does that make? Come on in all the same."

But St. Peter continued to bar the way. A mighty squabble ensued, and St. Joseph ended up saying to St.Peter, "Either you let him in, or I'm taking my wife and my boy and moving Paradise somewhere else."

His wife was our Lady, his boy our Lord. St. Peter thought it wiser to give in and admit the devotee of St Joseph.

- *Fava bean from St. Joseph altar should be carried for good luck and prosperity.*

Plutarch, the Greek writer (46ce-119ce) writes that Greeks and Romans held beans in high regard believing they had the capacity to invoke saints in times of need. In Sicily, the fava bean is credited with saving many from starvation being one of the few plants that thrived during a time of famine. Fava beans are roasted and handed out at St. Joseph Day altars having been blessed along with the altar and its many food offerings by a priest.

- *A small statue of St. Joseph can be buried in one's backyard to help sell their house.*

We know that Joseph was a carpenter, but few know that St. Joseph is the patron saint of fathers, expectant mothers, travelers, immigrants, craftsmen, engineers, working people, and house sellers and buyers. (www.catholic.org/saints/) Here is what Cheryl Dickow on the Catholic Exchange website says about burying a St. Joseph statute:

"When you (a Catholic) abide by the practices of our faith and never cross into superstition induced behavior, it could make perfect sense to bury a statue because it isn't the act of burying the statue that you see as having value and benefit but, instead, the intercession of St. Joseph, whom you rightfully call upon for help..." Now the question arises: Why bury St. Joseph? The Bible's mentioning of burying usually references death. However, the Bible's many references of sowing predominantly deal with reaping. It seems to make more sense that one should plant a statue of St. Joseph in the backyard to reap the goal of selling the house. Interestingly, many people report that after selling their house they go back to exhume St. Joseph, but are never able to find the statue. A curious end to this real estate transaction.

- *Use pictures of Jesus or the saints to calm a storm.*

Anthony DeBlasi shared an account of his mother's faith in the saints and in prayers to calm a storm. He writes, "Looking through the windows we saw an accelerating wind whip the trees immediately around us, in a circular motion. There was a strong sense that a mini-tornado was about to strike. It made mother recite *Lu Verbu*, a Sicilian prayer for safety in a storm. It begins:

> *Lu Verbu sacciu, lu Verbu a' ddiri,*
> *lu verbu chi lassau nostru Signuri*
> *quannu s'inniu a la cruci a muriri*
> *pi' sarvari a niatri piccaturi ...*

TRANSLATION:
I know The Verbu [a special "word" or incantation], I say The "Verbu,"
The "Verbu" that our Lord left us
when He went to die on the cross
to save us sinners ...

The dreaded whatever-it-was dissipated without further incident."
• *Pray to St. Anthony to find lost objects.*

> TONY, TONY ALL AROUND
> SOMETHING LOST
> MUST BE FOUND.

> DEAR ANTHONY
> PLEASE COME AROUND
> SOMETHING IS LOST
> THAT MUST BE FOUND

• *When you drop an article you must say:*

> *San Gerlando. Senza Dannu*

TRANSLATION:
Saint Garlando. Protect it from damage.

· SALT ·

- *If you wish that a person never returns, throw a pinch of salt at the back of his/her shoulders.*

This was considered a means to capture a witch, or at least stop her in her tracks by throwing salt on her shoulders. The axiom is somewhat related to the old belief that if one throws salt on a bird's tail it will immobilize the creature. Fearing the paralyzing effects of being hit with salt, and recalling Lot's wife's pillar of salt, one might be hesitant to return to a house where one bids them farewell by salting them.

- *Sprinkle salt on your door step for good luck and protection.*

- *When moving into another house, always bring a box of salt and a loaf of bread for good luck.*

- *Toss spilled salt over your left shoulder. Throwing it over your right shoulder will only bring on bad luck.*

- *Put salt around window sills to keep the devil out. He has to count every grain which will keep him too busy to enter.*

- *Sprinkle salt and water around your house to chase away evil demons.*

Salt was a valuable commodity in ancient Rome. Soldiers were paid with lumps of salt, *sal* in Latin. The good soldiers were called the "salt of the earth." The wages were called *salarium*, hence the English salary. Also, the Italian word for salt is *sale*. It probably isn't a coincidence that in these Roman times, salt was the currency used to barter. The exchange of money for goods is now considered a sale. It is understandable that spilling something this valuable would have been seen as an unlucky accident. To right the wrong, the person that spilled it would try to undo the bad luck by offering the spilled and presumably unusable salt over her/his left shoulder. Here again, the left side is considered the side that harbors the evil spirit, so the flying salt would chase away the demon. Sicilians would exclaim, "Mother of lightness" to ward off the ill effects of a spill. There is also the explanation that spilling salt represents the coming of bad things because Judas is depicted as knocking over the salt container at the last supper, and we know what followed that event. Salt is used as a deterrent to evil because it is considered pure and powerful; and, being found in the ocean, it is considered an earth element. Its whiteness intimates that it is a purifier, able to remove corruption, while it is itself incorruptible. In early times in Sicily, priests put a bit of salt in the child's mouth to impart wisdom.

· UMBRELLAS ·

- *It is unlucky to open an umbrella indoors.*

The word umbra means shadow, "excluding all light" (Merriam-Webster). This is the derivation of "umbrella". Believe it or not, the umbrella idea started in Egypt where there is little rain, but lots of sun. It was designed to shade people as its name implies. Its canopy shape suggested to Egyptians the body of a celestial goddess Nut. As such, its shade was sacred, meant only for the elite. If its shade should fall over a commoner, bad luck would befall the person (Panati). It is helpful to remember that later on, in the 1800 and beyond, the umbrella was a large black ribbed device unlike the small colorful umbrellas that one can fold and put in a suitcase today. The cruder devices had exposed wires that made up the ribs and indeed opening it in a small space inside was dangerous. Fully opened or even partially opened indoors, the umbrella becomes sinister, its sections resemble a black bat; and bats have always caused fear in most people. Outside, the opened umbrella does not take on the onus of darkness, or bad luck, but rather protection. One who purposefully opens one inside does so with little regard for others' feelings or safety and might incur their ill wills.

THE UMBRELLA FABLE
A Unique use of an Umbrella

In 1917, to drum up support for women's suffrage, Suffrage Headquarters used an umbrella to illustrate the silliness of denying women their right to vote. They placed an opened black umbrella with a large yellow bow in their window with signs all around it that read: "WOMEN SHOULD NOT BE PERMITTED TO USE UMBRELLAS BECAUSE

MEN ALREADY HAVE THEM. To let women have them too would only double expenses. THE WOMAN'S PLACE IS IN THE HOME. If she would stay away from stores, schools and churches when it rains, she would not need umbrellas. WOMEN CAN WALK UNDER THEIR HUSBANDS' UMBRELLAS. If They Have No Husbands, They Are to try to Get One Apiece, and Then They Can Walk Under Their Umbrellas. IF THEY ARE PERMITTED TO USE UMBRELLAS BY THEMSELVES WOMEN WILL NEGLECT THEIR HOMES. Because they can then gad about in the rain without getting wet. Moral: Women must not be permitted to Use Umbrellas" (p.16).

The Woman Citizen 1917 ended a pro-suffrage article with this short piece:

THE FIRST UMBRELLA

When the Man Who Invented the Umbrella Took It Out on the Streets of London, Years Ago, He Was Met with Jeers and Condemnation.

"What a Wicked Thing," People Said. "Did Not God Make the Rain to Rain Alike on the Just and the Unjust? This Man Is Blasphemous to Try to Keep Off the Rain from Heaven."

And Yet Today An Umbrella Is a Common-place Sight.

Woman Suffrage Has Had to Combat Just Such Unreasonable Prejudice.

Yet in a Few Years Women Will Be Voting All Over the United States and People will Think It Funny That Any Objection to Their Voting Was Ever Made.

VOTES FOR WOMEN (capitalization sic. page 16)

• WEDDINGS •

* *Steal a lemon from a St. Joseph Altar and bury it and you will be married within the year.*

I have an idea that there might be an inaccurate use of the word "steal" here. I suspect that one might discreetly "take" a lemon from the altar not nefariously "steal" one. In ancient Greece and Rome, the lemon tree was seen as a symbol of peace and well-being. Lemons were rare and so they were expensive in ancient Rome. Having them revealed an upper status class. In Christianity, the lemon tree is often included in paintings 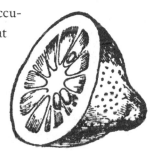 of the Virgin Mary presumably because of its sweet fragrance and healing properties. Since the lemon tree blooms and bears fruit throughout the year it is also associated with fidelity and fertility, two desirable elements in a marriage. It is also advantageous that the lemon on a St. Joseph altar is blessed along with everything else, so its potency is heightened all the more. (https://magickalspot.com/lemon-tree-symbolism-meaning).

* *Do not give knives as a wedding present.* (See **KNIVES**)

It would appear that giving a newly wedded couple knives, an instrument that cuts things apart would be an insensitive choice. Knives are tools of battles and destruction and to insinuate these often weapons into a new marriage would show poor timing not to mention, taste. It is probably best to let the newlyweds buy these household articles, unless they are heirloom parts of grandma's set and so handed down to the new generation.

- *The money dance with the bride is to donate money for the honeymoon, but also it is a means of wishing the couple continual prosperity.*

This is a well-known Italian custom, but it is also a custom in other countries as well. There are different ways of collecting the money while the bride and groom dance together. One way is to entrust an elder relative to hold *la borsa* (a fancy bag) and keep it available for guests to put donations into it; or more commonly, the wedding guests attach money to the bride's dress as the new couple dance. There are of course variations of this, for instance, male guests line up to dance with the bride and give her money as they dance with her while the groom dances with the ladies.

- *If even a sliver of one's petticoat shows under her skirt, the woman will soon find a husband.*

What is a petticoat? This is an old word for a slip. According to Lorrie Whittington, "[The petticoat] is a piece of lingerie that has finally had its day, and been relegated to the same class of obsolete underwear as the chemise and bloomers (or rather knickers...)" Since the above axiom mentions "one's petticoat", the saying must come from an era when showing the petticoat was considered "trashy", but kindlier, it would have seemed alluring to men. Perhaps the woman willingly allowed a sliver of her petticoat to show as she might have intentionally shown her ankle. Enticed by such brazenness, some men would have certainly sought to pursue her and thus create a relationship that eventually might lead to a marriage.

THE BRIDAL VEIL

The tradition of the bridal veil was intended to protect the bride from inadvertently making eye to eye contact with someone that is jealous or envious of her and wishes to cast an evil eye on her.

A TRADITIONAL ITALIAN WEDDING CUSTOM

After the wedding toast, the toast glasses are shattered while exclaiming, *cent'anni*, meaning "may your marriage last for a hundred years." The pieces of the glasses symbolize the number of years.

CARRYING THE BRIDE OF THE THRESHOLD

This custom is a relic of the Roman days of the captive brides. That is, when a Roman soldier wished to find a wife, he actually captured her. Here it was necessary to forcefully carry her over the threshold (Plutarch). (See *DOORS AND CHARMS*)

ABOUT ITALIAN WEDDINGS

Jerry Della Femina's book, *An Italian Grows in Brooklyn*, is a wonderfully instructive and humorous look at how things were growing up Italian during the 40's and 50's in his Brooklyn neighborhood. One of the funniest sections chronicles Italian weddings. He tells of the community's pressure (shopkeepers, priests, aunts, uncles) for any female over 21 to explain why she has not been married or why she has not planned to get married. There was always a sister, cousin, neighbor, someone given as an example of one who at the same age was married years ago. Louisa Calio illustrates these old country pressures when she writes about her Great-grandmother Rosa: "My mother said she [Rosa] felt guilty... for forcing her own daughter Millie to marry when she wanted to remain single and work at a lawyer's office. Millie married to please her mother and died a year later in childbirth..."

For the young couple that finally did plan to marry, the wedding reception was an affair to remember. Never would an invitation exclude the children. No matter the reception, there would always be children running about, participating in the festivities in their own ways. Della Femina describes the different scales of weddings: "Football weddings got their name from the fact that the main source of nourishment was sandwiches, made ahead of time, consisting usually of cheese, prosciutto, or provolone, and wrapped in waxed paper. The living room was cleared and two tables were set up at either end of the room. And then thousands of sandwiches would be heaped on the two tables." He adds these freely exposed sandwiches were "grabbed up with a vengeance." (p.133). Then there was the catered wedding. This was usually in a rented hall. Della Femina relates the time when the caterer tried to save money on waiters by setting up a buffet. "Gravesend simply wasn't ready for the concept of a buffet ... they really didn't know what to do with it. There were dozens of little old Italian men running from one end of the buffet table to the other uttering curses in Italian and saying in English 'What kind of place is this, with the food all piled up and the bread all piled up and nobody has taken the trouble to put it into sandwiches?'" (p.135).

Regarding the bride's dance with her father to the song "Daddy's Little Girl" and the groom's dance with his mother to "Mr. Wonderful", Della Femina writes, "The concept of the bride dancing with her father and the bridegroom with his mother is an image that touches all Italian bases. I can safely say that during the dancing of "Daddy's Little Girl" it never fails that Daddy weeps copiously..." (p.138).

In a personal memory, I recall a couple of aunts who always brought large handbags to the wedding receptions, stuffing left-overs into their bags lest the food go to waste or some relative who was unable to attend go without at least tasting a piece of wedding cake.

In a few closing words let me say that the relevance of these wedding memories and the forgoing axioms, proverbs, and "cures" is they call to mind snapshots of moments in our Italian upbringing that are, I suspect, more vivid in our minds than their original exposures. We were privileged to know and live these customs only because the old ones were still with us. They brought and followed the ways of the "old country" and prodded us to keep them going. As time has taken away these elders, practice of the traditions followed in their wake. Such is the nature of life. While realizing that all things must change, we second, third, fourth generation Italians, fondly remembering our childhoods, have a longing to recall and retell our memories and experiences in hopes that coming generations will be able to get some flavoring of what and how it was to be Italian "back then." Whether any, some, all, none of the proverbs and sayings here are efficacious is not quite the point of this writing. I suppose the point of this writing is to avoid representing these sayings and actions as the eccentricities of doddering old ones to be humored and dismissed, but rather to consider them as desperate means to control the care of loved ones and to shield them from the vagaries and dangers of a world that they, the elderly, had historically experienced as being unfriendly and unkind. In the final analysis, even if one judges these axioms as "superstitions," they do not detract from the richness of the Italians heritage. They are but a dimple in Italy's vast cultural fabric and add a unique seasoning to the ingredients that make us Italian.

THE STORIES
• •

ABOUT THE
STORIES' AUTHORS

• •

Vincentia Cacibauda (born August 1, 1917, Hern, Texas—died September 12, 2002, Belle Chasse, Louisiana) Vincentia Salsiccia Cacibauda is my mother. She rarely told us stories, so this one story of two gullible children giving away their mother's money is one I always remembered.

Italo Calvino (born 15 October, 1923, Santiago de Las Vegas, Cuba – died 19 September, 1985, Milan). Italian writer and journalist. His best-known works include the *Our Ancestors* trilogy (1952–1959), the *Cosmicomics collection of short stories* (1965), and the novels *Invisible Cities* (1972) and *If on a winter's night a traveler* (1979). Admired in Great Britain, Australia and the United States, he was the most translated contemporary Italian writer at the time of his death.

en.wikipedia.org/wiki/Italo_Calvino

Mrs. E.T. Corbett (born 1830, New York City—died 1899, New York City). Children's writer. Best known books are *Three Wise Old Women* and *Karl and the Queen of Queer-Land.*

www.wikii.org/en/29/wiki/writer/elizabeth-t-corbett-127547

Leonardo da Vinci (born 1452- died 1519) Artist, engineer, inventor, and scientist. Da Vinci scribbled short tales in the margins of his notes. The fables were found in his notebooks from the years 1487 to 1494. They are small imaginings of perhaps larger projects of higher thinking orders.

Medievalists.net

Antonio Fogazzaro (born in Vicenza, Italy, in 1842—died 1911, Italy) Italian novelist. Published his novel *Il Santo* (*The Saint*), which the Catholic Church deemed "heretical," in 1905. His most famous work was a trilogy of novels that were written about the "Risorgimento" or "War of Liberation" from the Austrian occupation of northern Italy.

Piccolo mondo antico made his reputation as leading writer. He was appointed to the Italian senate.

IMDb Mini Biography By: frankfob2@yahoo
www.imdb.com

Giovanni Francesco Straparola, (born c. 1480, Caravaggio, duchy of Milan [Italy]—died after 1557). Italian author of one of the earliest and most important collections of traditional tales. *Straparola's Piacevoli notti* (*The Nights of Straparola*) contains 75 novellas (short prose tales) that were later used as source material by William Shakespeare, Molière, and others. It drew from folk tradition and introduced into European literature some 20 fairy tales, among them what would eventually be known as *Beauty and the Beast* and *Puss in Boots*. Straparola's tales were drawn from many sources, and today some of his versions appear far removed from their present-day forms. Using a technique borrowed from Giovanni Boccaccio's Decameron, Straparola [blabber-mouth] set his stories within a frame. Each one is told on a successive night by a party of men and women relaxing at Murano, a suburb of Venice. His collection soon became famous throughout Europe."

www.britannica.com/biography/Gianfrancesco-Straparola

Antonio Ive (born August 13, 1851 in Rovinj, Croatia—died 1937 in Graz, Austria). An Austrian romance scholar and ethnologist of Italian origin. He headed the department of Italian language and literature at the University of Graz. The most important scientific works of Ive are connected with the history and current state of the North Italian dialects, especially those belonging to its native region, Istria [Croatian Peninsula], and with folklore monuments in these dialects. In 1879, he opened a manuscript of the Neapolitan version of the knightly novel *Fioravante* in the Paris National Library of the 14th century—a very important monument to the history of epic literature in Italy of the 15th and 16th centuries.

clever-geek.imtqy.com/articles/58066/index.html

Giacomo Leopardi (born June 29, 1798, Recanati, Papal States—died June 14, 1837, Naples) An Italian philosopher, poet, essayist, and philologist. "He is considered the greatest Italian poet of the nineteenth century and one of the most important figures in the literature of the world, as well as one of the principals of literary romanticism; his constant reflection on existence and on the human condition—of sensuous and materialist inspiration—has also earned him a reputation as a deep philosopher. He is widely seen as one of the most radical and challenging thinkers of the 19th century but routinely compared by Italian critics to his older contemporary Alessandro Manzoni despite expressing "diametrically opposite positions." Although he lived in a secluded town in the conservative Papal States, he came into contact with the main ideas of the Enlightenment, and, through his own literary evolution, created a remarkable and renowned poetic work, related to the Romantic era. The strongly lyrical quality of his poetry made him a central figure on the European and international literary and cultural landscape."

en.wikipedia.org/wiki/Giacomo_Leopardi
www.britannica.com/biography/Giacomo-Leopardi

Giuseppe Pitrè (Born December 22, 1841, Palermo—died April 10, 1916, Palermo) An Italian folklorist was also a medical doctor, professor, and senator in Sicily. As a folklorist he is credited with extending the realm of folklore to include all the manifestations of popular life. He was also a forerunner in the field of medical history. After serving as a volunteer in 1860 under Garibaldi, and graduating in medicine in 1866, Pitrè began researching and writing literature on Italian popular culture, which evolved into the quintessential Italian ethnographic studies. He founded the study of "folk psychology", in Sicily, teaching at the University of Palermo

Googlereads.com

Laura Elizabeth Howe Richards (born February 27, 1850, Boston, Massachusetts—died January 14,1943, Boston, Massachusetts) An American writer of the late 19th century who published more than 90 books. She wrote children's nonsense poems, her most famous called "Ele-telephony." Her mother was Julia Ward Howe, the lyricist for *The Battle Hymn of the Republic.*

www.poetry4kids.com/ news/ laura-e-richards-the-first-american-childrens-nonsense-poet/

CONTRIBUTORS

I am grateful to the many people who contributed to this work with writings and suggestions as to how I might go about putting it together. I thank all of the 400+ members of Facebook groups namely: I*talian American Writers Association, Arba Sicula, Bella Sicilia, New Orleans Italians, Italians of Louisiana, The Italian Group, Sicilian is a Language, We Are Italians, The Sicilian Group, Sicilian Respect, Williamson County Illinois Genealogy Group.* It is not possible to name the individuals, but I did record most of their names as they posted and tried to comment back with some information while tacitly appreciating all of their efforts.

There are also Italian and Sicilian writers who contributed to this work. Mark Hehl was very helpful to me having done this type of group gatherings from writers. He also contributed his own stories as part of my research. Giuseppe Cacciabaudo in Chiusa Sclafani, Palermo, Sicily also sent in writing and ideas and I thank Giuseppe for this. Louisa Calio, a wonderful poet, took time from her busy schedule and her writing to contribute a piece about her great-grandmother. Ettore Grillo, another great writer, in Enna, Sicily, graciously allowed me to use sections from his book, *A Hidden Sicilian History:* Second Edition. Then there are Richard Rotella, Anthony DeBlasi, and Josie Marino who sent material and kind words of encouragement to me. Thanks to these writers also. I also want to acknowledge Tiziano Thomas Dossena and Dominic Campanile for contributing their wonderful editing and graphic design skills.

A great public speaker used to say, "I don't mention names because I might eliminate somebody." Then he would begin to mention names. I know I am at risk of omitting someone here that deserves to be mentioned. In this event, I do apologize.

BIBLIOGRAPHY

- Benedict, Raphael. "The Origin of the Sign of the Cross." 9 September 2015. Catholicsay.com. https://catholicsay.com/the-origin-of-sign-of-the-cross/.

- Bergen, Fanny. "Some Siliva Charms." Journal of American Folklore, Volume 3 (1890). www.Archive.org.

- Bratley, George H. The Power of Gems and Charms. London: Gay and Bird, 1906. www.Archive.org.

- "Can Wet Hair Make You Sick?" February 2020. wwwmayoclinichealthsystem.org/hometown-health/speaking-of-health/can-wet-hair-make-you-sick. Accessed October 2021.

- Calvino, Italo. Italian Folktales. New York: Harcourt Brace Jovanovich, 1980.

- Carpenter, Edward. Pagan and Christian Creeds, Their Origin and Meaning. New York: Barcourt, Brace, and Howe Inc, 1920.

- Collison-Morley, Lacy. Greek and Roman Ghost Stories. London: Simpkin,Marshall and Company, 1911. Archives.org.

- Corbett, E.T. Karl and the Queen of Queer-Land. New York: American Book Exchange. 1880. www.Archive.org

- Cowie, Ashley. "Untwisting the Knotted History of Sea Witches." January 2018. www.ancient.origins.net. 2020.

- "Curative Properties of Potato." 2020. Offthegridnew.com. www.offthegridnews.com/alternative-health/curative-properties.

- Da Vinci, Leonardo. Fables of Leonardo da Vinci. Northbrook, Illinois: Hubbard Press. 1973

- Delaney, Gayle. In Your Dreams: Falling, Flying, and Other Dreams Themes. San Francisco: Harper, 1997.

- Della Femina, Jerry, Charles Sopkin. An Italian Grows in Brooklyn. Boston: Little Brown. 1978. www.Archive.org.

- "Discover the Meaning, Mystery, and Magic of Number 7." 2021. Numerologist.com/numerology/meaning-mystery-and-magic-of-the-number-7/.2021

- Douglas, Norman. Old Calabria. Gutenberg Project, 2003. www.gutenberg.org.

- Earth Element Symbolism. n.d. 2020. www.ancient-symbols.com/four-elements.html.

- Elworthy, Frederick Thomas. The Evil Eye: An Account of This Ancient and Wide Spread Superstition. New York: Bell Publishing, 1989.

- Fenin, Lily. "Seven Ways the Full Moon Supposedly Affects Your Body." 3 September 2016. Bustle.com. www.bustle.com/p/how-the-full-moon-supposedly-affects-your-body-3555343.

- Gambino, Richard. Blood of My Blood. Toronto, Buffalo: Guernica Editions, 1996.

- Gololo, S, et al. "Purification and Characterization of Proteases from Cow Dung." The Annals of Fires and Burn Disaster XXXII(2) (July 2019). www.researchgate.net.

- Grillo, Ettore. A Hidden Sicilian History: Second Edition (p. 54). Strategic Book Publishing & Rights Co. Kindle Edition.

- Hall, James. The Sinister Side: How Left-Right Symbolism Shaped Western Art. New York: Oxford Press, 2008.

- Hall, Maggie J. "What Are the Medical Uses of Coal Oil." 2020. Wisegeek.com. https://www.wisegeek.com/what-are-the-medical-uses-of-coal-oil.htm.

- Hastings, James, et al. "Charms and Amulets from The Encyclopaedia of Religion and Ethics: Volume III." 2020. Archive.com. www.archive.org.

- "Healing Power of Olive Oil, The." 19 December 2016. Kasandrinos.com. www.kasandrinos.com/blogs/news/the-healing-power-of-olive-oil-1.

- Heaton, Elizabeth. By-Paths in Sicily. New York: E.P. Dutton, 1920. www.gutenberg.org.

- "History of the Broom, The." 11 March 2010. The Pagan's Path. paganspath.com/magik/broom.htm.

- Hood, Alexander Nelson. Sicilian Studies. London: George Allen & Unwin Ltd. Rushin House, 1915. www.archive.org.

- "How Does the Moon Affect Your Body." 2020. Almanac.com.

- Ive, Antonio. "The Love of Three Oranges." (p.338). Italian Popular Tales. Thomas F. Crane. Boston:Houghton, Mifflin and Co. 1885. Archives.org.

- Law-Rence, Robert Means. Magic of the Horse-Shoe with Other Folk-lore Notes. Boston, New York: Houghton Mifflin & Co., 1898. www.gutenberg.org/files/57411/57411-h/57411-h.htm.

- Leopardi, Giacomo. "Dialogue Between the Earth and the Moon" (p.42). Essays and Dialogues. Translated by Charles Edwardes. London: Trubner and Company. 1882. Project Gutenberg. January 2021.

- "Limbo: Origin and Meaning of Limbo." 2020. Online Etymonline.com.https://www.etymonline.com/word/limbo.

- Lloyd, Deborah, Reiki Master. "Right Side vs. Left Side Energies." May 2015. Reiki Rays. 2020. reikirays.com/22216/right-side-vs-left-side-energies.

- Mandell, Judy. "Why We Feel Compelled to Say 'Bless You' When Someone Sneezes." 7 September 2019. The New York Times. www.nytimes.com/2019/09/17/well/mind/sneezing-sneezes-god-bless-you-manners-etiquette.html.

- Mangione, Jerre. Mount Allegro: A Memoir of Italian American Life. New York: Crown Publishers, Inc.,1972.

- Ogle, M.B. "The House Door in Greek and Roman Religion and Folk Lore." 1911. JSTOR. The American Journal of Philology. www.jstor.org.

- Park, Roswell. The Evil Eye Thanatology and Other Essays. Boston: The Gorham Press, 1912.

- Pavitt, W.T. and K. Pavitt. "Talismans Past and Present." JSTOR Journal:The Lotus Magazine, Volume 9. (1918). archive.org/details/jstor-20544049/mode/2up.

- Perl, Lila. Don't Sing Before Breakfast, Don't Sleep in the Moonlight. New York: Clarion Books, 1988.

- Potter, Carole. Knock on Wood: An Encyclopedia of Talismans, Charms, Superstitions, and Symbols. New York, Toronto: Beaufort Books, Inc., 1983.

- Ramond, Chris. "Superstitions About Death and Dying." 28 June 2018. Liveabout.com. www.liveabout.com/13-superstitions-about-death-and-dying-1132083.

- Richards, Laura E. The Pig Brothers and Other Fables and Stories (page 67). Boston: Little, Brown, and Company. 1932. Gutenberg.org. Accessed October, 2021.

- Sass, Cynthia,. "Seven Benefits of Oranges, According to Nutritionists." 19 February 2021. Explore Health. www.health.com/food/health-benefits-oranges.

- Simpson, Jacqueline. European Mythology. New York: P.Bedrick Books, 1987. Archive.org.

- Sven Tito, Achen. Symbols Around Us. New York: Van Sostrand Reinhold, 1978.

- "Teeth Falling Out Dream: The Interpretation and Meaning Revealed." 24 November 2020. msn.com. www.msn.com/en-us/lifestyle/horoscope/teeth-falling-out-dream-dream-interpretation-and-meaning-revealed/arBB11TNuZ?fullscreen=true#image=1.

- "Umbrella Fable, The." The Women Citizen Journal, 1917. Volume 1. Kahle/Austen Foundation. Archives.org. Accessed October 26, 2021.

- Wallis-Budge, E.A. Amulet and Superstitions. London: Oxford Press, 1930.

- Waring, Philippa. The Dictionary of Omens and Superstitions. Sacaucus, New Jersey: Chartwell Books, 1986.

- "Why Do You Throw Salt Over Your Shoulder?" 23 March 2019. Astonishing Legends. 2020. www.astonishinglegends.com/astonishing-legends/2019/3/23/why-do-you-throw-salt-over-your-shoulder.

- Wilde, Lady. Ancient Legends, Mysteries, Charms, and Superstitions. Boston: Ticknor and Company, 1887.

INDEX OF CONTENTS

• •

coal oil: 64, 155

color(s): 19, 33-34, 79, 82, 109

comb: 58, 118

cornu: 82

cow manure (healing properties): 65

cupping: 61

curse(s): 19, 51, 59, 79, 82, 87, 142

      neighbor's: 25

day(s): 5, 35-38, 39, 53-54, 71, 83, 94, 100, 114, 141

death: 7-8, 10, 12, 18, 21, 33-34, 39-40, 44, 47, 53-55, 89-90, 108,
      114, 131, 147, 157

dish towel: 41

dog howling: 7

door(s): 2-3, 25, 27, 43-45, 55, 72, 81, 94-95, 110, 127, 133

doorway(s): 17, 43, 45, 72, 95, 127, 141

dream(s): 40, 47, 154

drinking and eating: 24, 31, 37, 49, 55, 61, 85, 90, 95, 112, 117, 119, 125

evil eye: see *malocchio*

evil spirit(s): 10, 21, 27, 44-45, 55, 72, 111, 121

fig tree: 12-13, 51-52

forks: 73-75

Friday: 17, 36, 44, 53-55, 63, 69, 77, 81, 90

funerals: 9, 17, 39, 43, 113

      wash clothes: 36, 70

garlic: III, 10, 25, 63, 66, 80

      pinned to a baby's shirt: 10

JOSEPH L. CACIBAUDA
● ●

Joseph L. Cacibauda is a retired musician and elementary school teacher living in Reno, Nevada with his wife Sue. Joe has written five books, two published by Legas Press, New York, on Sicilian Immigrants and three published on Amazon about musicians. He has written for the Sons and Daughters of Italy magazine, *Italian America*, the Arba Sicula Sicilian Society's Journal, *Sicilian Dawn* and its magazine, *Sicilia Para*, as well as contributed book reviews to online blogs and magazines. Joe's other works are included in two collections of stories by Italian writers, *Ameri-Sicula: Sicilian Culture in America*, Legas Press, New York; and *A Feast of Narrative*, Idea Press, Florida. Joe is a second-generation Sicilian-American, very interested in researching and writing about early Sicilian and Italian ways and traditions. He hopes his writings helps nurture respect for these cultures and spurs an interest in readers to learn more.

Made in the USA
Las Vegas, NV
16 November 2022

59674631R00111